Frontier Children

FRONTIER
CHILDREN

Linda Peavy & Ursula Smith
Foreword by Elliott West

UNIVERSITY OF OKLAHOMA PRESS / NORMAN

Also by Linda Peavy and Ursula Smith

Women Who Changed Things (New York, 1983)
Dreams into Deeds (New York, 1985)
*The Gold Rush Widows of Little Falls: A Story
    Drawn from the Letters of Pamelia and James
    Fergus* (St. Paul, Minn., 1990)
*Women in Waiting in the Westward Movement:
    Life on the Home Frontier* (Norman, 1994)
*Pioneer Women: The Lives of Women on the
    Frontier* (New York, 1996; Norman, 1998)

Printed and bound in Hong Kong
by C&C Offset Printing Co., Ltd.

Below: *Some of the sharpest extant images of frontier children were promotional photos taken by commercial photographers like Albert Schlecten of Bozeman, Montana. Schlecten frequently used youngsters to add interest and perspective to scenes depicting the bounty of a Gallatin Valley harvest or the beauty of life in the Rocky Mountain West.*

Library of Congress Cataloging-in-Publication Data

Peavy, Linda S.
Frontier children / by Linda Peavy, Ursula Smith; fore-
    word by Elliott West.
        p.   cm.
    Includes index.
    ISBN 0-8061-3161-6 (cloth: alk. paper)
    1. Pioneer children—West (U.S.)—History—19th
    century. 2. Frontier and pioneer life—West (U.S.)
    3. West (U.S.) —Social life and customs—19th cen-
    tury. 4. West (U.S.)—Social conditions—19th cen-
    tury.
    I. Smith, Ursula. II. Title.
    F956.P398   1999
    978—dc21   99–18932
                                                    CIP

The paper in this book meets the guidelines for perma-
nence and durability of the Committee on Production
Guidelines for Book Longevity of the Council on Library Resources, Inc. ∞

2 3 4 5 6 7 8 9 10

For

Lauren, Beatrice,

Henry, Isaiah,

Sarah, and Hannah,

children of the New West

Right: *Through three sea-sons of the year, little Wyoma Henry, named for her native state, lived with her parents in a sheep wagon whose cramped interior was furnished with a sturdy wood-burning stove, ca. 1902.*

CONTENTS

Foreword

by Elliott West

Linda Peavy and Ursula Smith lead us into two territories that are both intimate and alien. The first is the American frontier, which haunts our memory as a place of national beginnings. We imagine that its tribulations, accomplishments, horrors, and misdeeds shaped our collective character, both for better and worse. The second territory is that of individual origins—our childhoods. We form our personal myths, the stories that explain who we are, through remembered moments from the age of seven or twelve. Perhaps it was a perfect birthday or when our dog died, the first twenty yards ridden on a bicycle, this or that humiliation or victory. Like our selected frontier episodes, these personal memories shaped us, we believe; and so they are still with us.

Yet we are also reminded constantly of how far we have traveled from those beginnings. Pioneer ox wagons and dugouts might as well be from a distant continent when we look back from our days in suburbia and nights of cable television. Even as we imagine our kinship to the frontier by borrowing its names, we mock ourselves by what we give them to: "Mustangs" are flashy cars that zip along superhighways; "ranch style" houses have microwave ovens, personal computers, and garbage disposals. And any adult who pays attention knows that children are foreign creatures. We glimpse how they see the world, and we stand slack-jawed. As a parent I often feel that I have more in common with a Kurdish villager or a member of the Thai royal family than with my sons and daughters who share our Saturday night hamburgers.

Frontier Children captures beautifully that tension between identity and strangeness. Like Peavy and Smith's earlier book, *Pioneer Women*, it combines a wide ranging historical description with a stunning collection of images. The subjects this time are characters who have been, if anything, even more neglected in the standard treatments of the frontier West. *Frontier Children* shows us how much we have been missing. Peavy and Smith have arranged their chapters almost as a story. Beginning with the children's movement to and around the frontier, they take us through the natural and domestic worlds where they grew up, their working lives and playtime, their schooling, and finally their passages toward adulthood.

Each part resonates in our memory; each is a trip into the Land of Odd. Amusements are full of echoes from everyone's early years. Indian children play with spinning tops made from acorns, and New Mexican boys spend hours as horses clopping on all fours, hooved with milk cans. And next to these, the jarringly different: Sioux boys compete in a game with teams throwing flaming torches at one another. Sons and daughters work at household chores and baby-sitting, but then we are out alone with the six Wormer girls on the Republican River of Kansas as they trap and skin skunks, bobcats, and badgers. Three states to the north, a German-Russian father hires out his son and daughter as draft animals for a thresher. The mix of the familiar and the hard-to-imagine runs throughout. Children on the overland trails marvel at the sights and get bored, like modern summer vacationers, yet eleven-year-old Elisha Brooks drives his family's four-oxen wagon all the way to Oregon.

It is especially satisfying to find an array of cultures in these accounts. The frontier was not a single line of pioneer settlement moving steadily westward across the continent, but rather an often chaotic mingling and collision of many peoples. Peavy and Smith bring Chinese, Hispanics, Paiutes, African Americans, Sioux, and Sheepeaters into a story too often reserved for east-to-west European Americans. While pioneer youngsters were learning multiplication and history at school, Indian children practiced planting corn with a stick and listened to elders' stories that instilled courage and self-discipline. A Montana homesteader's daughter, wholly uninformed at her first menses, was given a cloth and a few curt instructions. A Navajo girl followed a four-day ritual, beginning with a long dawn run as she chanted, "The breeze coming from her is beautiful." By allowing so many voices, Peavy and Smith give us a far more accurate and convincing view of the frontier; the cultural spread adds as well to the overall impression, the simultaneous feel of the recognizable and the exotic.

If the stories engage us, the remarkable photographs pull us further into the frontier children's world. A thorough combing of archives gave Peavy and Smith a range of images, and as in the text, it is a diverse bunch we see: boxcar dwellers and Hispanic corn-huskers, youthful slayers of mountain lions, orphans, Great Basin Indians by their wickiup, Crow sisters in dresses spangled with elk teeth, and mining-camp youngsters costumed from the eighteenth

century, presumably in a historical pageant. As was usual in that time, the photographs often show a posed family or group. We lose almost all sense of action, but in the stillness are advantages: we are drawn to imagine what we have interrupted. A Methodist missionary stands behind several solemn Kiowa girls. In front of them all is his bicycle. A lesson, maybe? When he left, did the children laugh at him as The Preacher Who Pedals? If we could talk to the family of freed slaves, Exodusters, who wait for a steamboat to take them west, what would they tell us of where they came from? What pictures of the Kansas plains are in the head of that boy asleep on the pile of blankets? In ways that only a picture conveys, we are reminded over and over of the unbridgeable gap between our children's concerns and our own. Two dirty-faced girls hold hands and smile playfully at the photographer. Their parents were among the desperate strikers in the Colorado coalfields in 1913–14 locked in a brutal confrontation that ended in the Ludlow Massacre.

And there are the faces. The expressions are of young people expected to grow up fast. Nearly everyone seems set at serious business. Typically the looks are direct and unsmiling, except among those too young to have learned a respectable sternness, like the Montana baby contestants, terrified and astonished at where they find themselves. Yet even among the older children something at the edges of the eyes often gives them away. We see a curiosity at the commonplace, or a fearful unease over being plopped in the middle of one more situation grown-ups have created, or a giggle trying to happen. And we recognize the universal experience of the young, that country from which we adults are in permanent exile. The surroundings are other frontier situations that we somehow know, but also know we have left behind us: a logging-camp dance in northern California, Apache children and their mothers under armed guard, a boy and a girl beside a mining-camp sluice, and two boys clearing an Oregon field with an ox-drawn stone boat.

The experiences of frontier children are a distinctively American variation of what draws us to all history—both the need to stand on the common ground of the human condition and the desire to enter experiences utterly strange. We can thank Linda Peavy and Ursula Smith for taking us on this compelling trip into fascinating terrain.

Below: For the children of Judge J.H. McCleary, camping in the Mammoth Hot Springs area of Yellowstone National Park was a highlight of the summer of 1887.

Frontier Children

The Infinite Variety

Childhood on the Frontier

Any mention of childhood on the American frontier readily brings to mind familiar, if stereotypical, images: an Indian infant securely laced in its cradleboard, a tow-headed youngster bathed in shadows from a campfire, a barefoot student at a crude desk in a prairie schoolhouse. Yet beyond these stock impressions, most readers have little knowledge of the actual day-to-day experiences of frontier children.

The relative paucity of information on childhood in the trans-Mississippi West is surprising, when one considers that children were as integral a part of frontier life as were adults. They were evident in every Indian clan and village, on every hacienda, in every mining camp, on every homestead, and in every town. Their presence was, indeed, a major impetus for giving formal structure to frontier society. And yet children have remained all but invisible in the historic record.

This gap in our knowledge was pointed out some twenty-five years ago by historian Ruth Moynihan. After examining the reminiscences of adults who had made the overland journey in childhood, she became convinced of the need for further work in this area, reminding us that "history is made by children as well as by adults and impersonal forces."[1] In the years since her 1975 article appeared, a number of studies on frontier childhood have begun to replace some of the old stereotypical images with flesh-and-blood figures.[2]

The Sources

The sources used in such studies have been hard to come by, primarily because so few letters and journals written by children survive. Early nineteenth-century writings by Indian children in the trans-Mississippi West are virtually nonexistent, since most of those children had no written language of their own. Indeed, only after Indian children were removed from their native environment and taught the English language in government and mission schools did they begin to leave written records. Our knowledge of the childhood experiences of the earliest inhabitants of the American West is therefore largely limited to what we can extrapolate from pictographs; from generic stories handed down orally from generation to generation; from the journals of trappers, explorers, and missionaries; and from the drawings and paintings done by artists from an alien culture.

Opposite: The children of American Horse, on the Pine Ridge Reservation, South Dakota, ca. 1908. The influence of white settlers on the lives of these Lakota children is evident from the log cabin and corral in the background and from their clothing—braids, beads, furs, and moccasins worn with jeans and knit shirts.

Below: One of the earliest depictions of a tipi interior, this Peter Rindisbacher painting of a Plains Indian family group presents a highly stylized view of native life.

> Ros ebvrg Ogn Faily. 13. 1862
>
> Dear Pa pa I did not write the last time when George did I have been three months to School to Miss Sloan Pa I wish you wold write to me and tel me when you are coneing hone fore I should like to no I run a nail in my foot and Jcant walk on it Pa I uant you to come home I ~~uat~~ uant to ~~see~~ see you right bad
>
> from your son Loyal

Above: A letter from nine-year-old Loyal Stearns of Roseburg, Oregon, to his father in the Salmon River mines, July 13, 1862. Although relatively rare, letters of frontier children provide a child's-eye view of life in the West.

be constructed largely from later-life memoirs and oral history transcripts. This adult view of childhood has the advantage of providing a somewhat more comprehensive account than would be provided by a young child caught up in the day-to-day activities of frontier living. However, adult reminiscences—whether written or oral—lack the immediacy of diaries and letters. Furthermore, historians are wisely wary of the accuracy of reports composed so many years after the fact—softened or hardened as such writings inevitably are by the passage of time and shaded as they often are by the author's need to verify or contradict accounts written by fellow pioneers or by the desire to entertain and astound the reader.

These limitations aside, the cumulative weight of detail in adult reminiscences of childhood can be relied upon to provide us with some idea of what it was like to grow up on the western frontier. Furthermore, the stories told in reminiscences can be set against quantitative and qualitative information found in vintage newspapers, in

Predictably, there were virtually no written records left behind by the children of African ancestry who walked across the continent with their mothers, following the wagons of their owners. Even freed blacks left scant evidence of what it was like to be a child in the West, but considering how few slaves had been given the opportunity to learn to read and write, one would not expect to find an abundance of journals written by African Americans who moved west following emancipation. And the scarcity of English translations of letters and diaries written by children who came to the American West from Europe, Asia, and Mexico should also not be surprising, given the difficulty of finding personal writings by the children of even English-speaking westering families.

In the face of such limited access to the writings of the children themselves, the stories of childhood on the frontier must

Right: Dressed in their best and patiently holding their pose, unidentified Gallatin Valley, Montana, brothers stare impassively into the photographer's lens, ca. 1900.

local and regional histories, and in such public records as census rolls and court documents.

Reminiscences can also be corroborated—or countered—by photographic evidence, a large body of which began to be amassed in the last half of the nineteenth century. Indeed, given the sparseness of the written record, the photographic record of childhood on the frontier is unexpectedly extensive. This anomaly is explained, in part, by the fact that the daguerreotype was developed in 1839, at about the same time pioneering families were beginning to leave loved ones for new homes in the West. The discovery that an image could be permanently captured and shared with those left

behind inspired many a doting parent to pay the fee required by an itinerant photographer—or to take the child, dressed in Sunday best, to a newly established studio in a nearby settlement. Not coincidentally, the new art of photography also enabled the development of a visual record of life in Indian encampments at a time when that life was being threatened with extinction.

It is from such sources—from the relatively few extant letters and diaries of frontier children, from adult reminiscences, from public and private records that mention children, and from vintage photographs—that historians have begun to reconstruct the stories of childhood in the West.

Above: *In this northern California variant of the classic school picture, scholars and their teachers pose on a giant redwood stump, ca. 1900.*

Right: *A turn-of-the-century Wyoming mother and three of her children pose in the hay mow as an amateur photographer—perhaps her own son—tries his luck with a bellows-focus camera. With the introduction of faster film and simple box cameras that required less tedious focusing, scenes such as this were soon to become relatively commonplace.*

The Photographer's Art

The importance of the photograph to the frontier family is evident in lines from a letter written in 1878 by a proud young mother living in the Madison Valley of Montana Territory. "We went down Saturday in the forenoon to get the babies picture," Nellie Fletcher wrote to her family in the East. "She was very good. The artist kept talking to her and whistling to attract her attention."[a]

Though the photograph itself has been lost to time, a mother's pride in being able to share her child's likeness with loved ones back home remains a matter of written record. Fortunately for researchers, thousands of other frontier parents were equally interested in utilizing the new science of photography to document the lives of their children.

The development of photography paralleled the settlement of the American West. The earliest photographs were displayed in France in the summer of 1839, a scant two years before the wagons first began to roll west from outposts on the Missouri and the Mississippi. And by the end of the following decade photography had reached the American West itself. During the 1850s photographers set up shop in fledgling settlements all across the frontier, advertising their services through newspapers and flyers. Itinerant photographers rode from homestead to homestead, providing pioneer families with on-site documentation of the particulars of their new life. Even homesteaders like the Fletchers, who had little money to spare, were more than willing to pay for a priceless photograph.

Making a "likeness" was not an easy art—for either the photographer or the subject. Cameras were big and bulky, and the large glass plates required to capture the image were hard to handle and had to be chemically treated immediately before insertion into—and immediately after removal from—the camera. And since early daguerreotypes and even photographs made as late as the early years of the twentieth century required long exposure times, posing for a picture took patience and steady nerves—qualities not usually associated with children.[b]

Although highly prized by frontier families, by their descendants, and by latter-day archivists and researchers, vintage photographs can easily convey a false impression of childhood in the West. Children in early studio portraits often appear against an artificial backdrop, posed with toys or other props that were not necessarily a part of their lives. The children seen in pictures taken by traveling photographers are usually dressed in their very best clothing, which may or may not have been appropriate to the situation or setting. Native American children are also clearly out of their element in posed portraits, pictured as they often are in ceremonial dress, impassively staring at the photographer.

Such contrived images have their place, but our understanding of childhood on the frontier is immeasurably enriched by the more natural and spontaneous images of childhood to be found in the photographic record. Our eye is caught—and our imagination engaged—by the stark image of a child staring at the camera from the back of an Indian pony, from the sunlit doorway of a settler's soddy, or from the littered yard of a mining shanty. We are moved even more by the image of a child laid out in its coffin, painful testament to a parent's irreplaceable loss. Whatever the image, such pictorial evidence is an invaluable aid in reconstructing and conveying the history of childhood on the frontier.

---

[a] Patricia Dean, "Children in Montana," *Montana The Magazine of Western History* 34 (Winter 1984): 45.

[b] Russell Freedman, *Children of the Wild West* (New York: Clarion, 1983), 9–10.

Above: *Little William Andrews Marshall of Denver, Colorado, was posed in a washbowl, a favorite prop of photographers in the 1880s.*

Above: U.S. cavalrymen guard a group of Apache women and children taken prisoner during a raid on their village. A southwestern tribe, the Apaches were considered "hostile" Indians, and their children often suffered ill treatment at the hands of enemy tribes and the federal government.

Right: Keeping a tight grip on her nursing bottle helped this Helena, Montana, child hold still for her turn-of-the-century portrait.

The Stories

The stories are highly individual. For some who grew up on the frontier, childhood was—or was recalled as—an idyllic time of love, laughter, and security, a time of carefree adventure in a nurturing world. For others it was a harsh struggle for survival in an isolated and punishing environment. And, for still others, it was a period marred by the invasion of one's homeland and the destruction of a way of life.

Frontier Children pays tribute to the many and varied aspects of growing up in the West. It explores the world of Native American youngsters born into a century that brought rapid and radical change. It examines the bicultural worlds of the Hispanic children of the Southwest and the privileged children of the Californios. It details the experiences of the children who crossed the continent by land or by water to settle in new homes in Kansas and Colorado, in California and Oregon. And it looks at ways in which the children of Asian and European immigrants adjusted to their new lives in West Coast cities, on the plains of the Dakotas, and in the mining towns of the Rockies.

Left: The Victorian family model, as typified by the Emmett Bryant family of Santa Maria, California, ca. 1880. The father, proprietor of a local hardware store, concerned himself with the world of commerce, while the mother, Laura Sharp Bryant, was responsible for the home and the children—Lucille, Ruby, and Elwood.

The Context

The stories told in these pages should, ideally, be read with at least a cursory understanding of the philosophical and sociological views of childhood held by nineteenth-century American society— or more appropriately, societies, for these views differed according to culture and circumstance.

In most Native American cultures children were viewed as both a blessing and a responsibility, and the child's care and training were shared by the extended family—grandparents, aunts, uncles, and elder siblings as well as parents—if not by the whole clan.[3] Although there were situations in which Indian children lived under less-than-optimum conditions, in most tribes, the child was indulged and allowed to grow to maturity with relatively little responsibility and an abundance of free play that served as early training for his or her role in adulthood.

Among many westering nineteenth-century families, views of childhood were largely informed by Victorian attitudes. The "cult of true womanhood," which set forth the standards of piety, purity, passiv-

ity, and domesticity for women, had its corollary in the "cult of the child," which established the standards for a healthy, wholesome childhood. According to the Victorian ideal, the child was viewed not as a miniature adult, as children had been perceived in an earlier era, but as an innocent who was to enjoy a life of carefree happiness until he or she grew old enough to assume the responsibilities of a strictly gendered adult role.[4]

Under this model, the mother was given almost total charge of the upbringing of the children, and she followed well-established guidelines for their education, religious training, discipline, diet, clothing, and exercise. The father, the family's titular head, its breadwinner, and its contact with the outside world, was only minimally engaged in the daily lives of his wife and children.

The Victorian model of ideal family life had, of course, little relevance for those families in which mothers, by virtue of circumstance, worked outside the home and depended on their oldest children to carry on the basic chores of the house-

Above: *A girl, her two brothers, and their two dogs were posed by a photographer in landlocked Butte, Montana Territory, in front of a backdrop depicting a home on some distant rocky shore.*

Right: *Six months old in 1875, Alice Clare Dahler of Virginia City, Montana Territory, was dressed in her finest to have her picture "struck" to send to family "back home."*

hold—including caring for themselves and their younger siblings. Nor did it apply to poverty-stricken immigrants eking out a living in eastern cities and, as a matter of necessity, sending their children to work in the mills, collect rags in the streets, or beg in the marketplace. The model also failed to take into account the particular circumstances of rural families in which mothers and children worked the fields alongside the men of the household.[5]

Irrelevant as it was to the realities of the majority of American households, the Victorian notion of childhood as an age of innocence and play followed many Anglo middle-class families west. However, "the cult of the child"—like "the cult of true womanhood"—generally underwent speedy and sweeping revisions in the face of the hardships of westward emigration and of life on the frontier. Indeed, many children who settled in the West were performing important indoor and outdoor chores by the time they were five years old, and most children were full participants in the workforce by the age of fifteen or sixteen.[6]

Hard work from an early age was the rule for the children of most of the European immigrants who sought a new life on the American frontier. The German-Russians who settled North Dakota generally brought with them from their homeland the centuries-old perception of children as small adults who were to be held to the same standards as their elders. Discipline was strict, work was hard, and play was not a distinct or honored component of daily life.[7]

In contrast, one researcher of Hispanic family life has remarked on the air of "splendor and freedom" that permeated adult reminiscences of childhood on the rancho, though it is not hard to imagine exceptions to this view. In Californio and other Hispanic families the father was the dominant figure, but both parents were responsible for instilling the virtues of respect, obedience, and humility from an early age. As the children matured, the father took over the training of his sons and

the mother assumed responsibility for the training of her daughters, thereby heightening the distinctions in their gendered adult roles and responsibilities.[8]

The particulars of child rearing among westering black families remains, for the most part, shrouded in mystery. Most likely, the practices of parents caught in the generations-old web of slavery owed as much to the mores forced upon them by their owners as to the traditions handed down by their African ancestors. However,

adult reminiscences of the Exodusters who settled in Kansas in the wake of Reconstruction would suggest that the work and play of their childhood was touched by the hope of a new life that had drawn their parents west, a hope that remained steadfast even in the midst of the day-to-day struggle for survival in the small, transitory settlements they came to know as home.[9]

For the relatively small number of Chinese children in the trans-Mississippi West, life had few elements of the typical

Right: *High-caste mothers and daughters of Chinatown in late-nine-teenth-century Los Angeles.*

American childhood. Female children were held to be of little or no value in Chinese culture, and young, even pre-adolescent, girls were sometimes sold by their families in China to traders supplying bordellos on the West Coast and in the gold camps. Late in the century, after the Chinese Exclusion Act of 1882 restricted immigration of female Chinese to the wives of Chinese merchants already established in the United States, Chinese family life began to stabilize in various "Chinatowns." Raised in the isolation of an enclosed society, the children of these families knew a life that was similar in many ways to the life that they would have known back in the homeland, a life in which women—and therefore girls—led very proscribed lives and boys prepared themselves to follow the trades of their fathers, which in America were generally limited to those of merchant, cook, laundryman, or laborer.[10]

As this brief overview has suggested, childhood on the American frontier is a far more complex topic than might first be supposed, and a comprehensive treatment of all aspects of the topic is clearly beyond the scope of any one book. *Frontier Children* is essentially a verbal and visual montage that celebrates the experiences of children growing up in the American West. The infinite variety of those experiences can be seen in vivid snippets drawn from the letters, journals, and memoirs of those who lived the stories we write and in the images that amplify those stories—the vintage sketches, paintings, and photographs that are monuments to a moment in the rich and varied lives of frontier children.

Above: A toddler clutching her rattle caught by the camera in the sunlit doorway of her Montana home, ca. 1880.

Ebb and Flow

Frontier Children on the Move

For the children of the various tribes who first populated the Great Plains, travel was a way of life. Indeed, migration was an integral part of the heritage of these tribes. Their ancestors had crossed the Bering Strait from Asia some thirty thousand years before, and by the fourteenth century the descendants of these early immigrants had occupied the whole of the North American continent, establishing trading and hunting routes, tribal alliances, and, in some cases, elaborate agricultural enterprises. But by the mid-nineteenth century the challenges posed by successive invasions of Europeans had inexorably reduced the free-roaming American Indians to the unclaimed portions of the Great Plains, the desertlands of the Southwest, and the coastal plains of the Pacific slope. The peoples of the latter two regions and the Mandans to the north continued to enjoy their centuries-old pueblo- or village-based cultures while the hunters and gatherers among the native peoples of the plains continued to move from camp to camp according to season and circumstance.

Though migration was a given for the children of many Plains Indians, it was a historic experience—in many cases, a singular adventure—for the half million or so settlers' children who journeyed west in the nineteenth century.[1] Most of these young emigrants crossed the continent by wagon and later by rail. Some steamed south out of Boston, New York, Charleston, or New Orleans to cross the Isthmus or round the Horn on their way to California. Still others traveled west in Missouri River steamers. However they went, they accompanied parents drawn by dreams of gold or free land—or by the opportunity to begin anew.

Native Children on the Move

Alongside their elders, the children of the Plains Indians followed the seasonal migrations of the animals they hunted, moving between their summer encampments and their winter villages. The long marches, the assembling and dismantling of tipis and huts, the excitement—and discomforts—of life on the trail were standard fare for the Osage, Sioux, or Cheyenne child.

These migrations, based on generations of practice, were highly organized affairs that took into account the needs of all members of the tribe or clan, even the youngest. On long marches, infants were

Opposite: *Three children and their dog on the Mormon Trail in the 1860s.*

Below: *In this undated photo, the children of the Stump Horn family are preparing for a journey across the plains of eastern Montana—with cradleboarded baby in its mother's arms, toddlers safely ensconced within the travois, and older children walking alongside.*

Above: *The wagons depicted in Robert Lindneux's painting* The Trail of Tears *were actually a very rare sight on this forced march over eight hundred miles. Most men, women, and children made the nine-month journey on foot through the fall, winter, and spring of 1838–39. The original painting hangs in the Woolaroc Museum in Bartlesville, Oklahoma.*

The Trail of Tears

While the migrations of the Plains Indians were a lifestyle fostered by habit and environment, the forced removal of the Cherokee in 1838–39 from their homelands in the southern Appalachians to Indian Territory—present-day Oklahoma—was an aberration in that people's history.

In the early summer of 1838, President Andrew Jackson—who acted in defiance of the Supreme Court's decision in favor of the tribe—ordered army troops to force some eighteen thousand Cherokee men, women, and children from their homes. Herded at bayonet point into "removal forts" in Georgia, Arkansas, Tennessee, and North Carolina, the Indians were organized into "detachments" that often separated children from their parents. In midsummer the first of these detachments began a three-month passage by steamboat and barge along the Tennessee and Ohio Rivers to the Mississippi, and thence up the Arkansas River into Indian Territory.

That October, at about the same time the first riverboat detachments reached Oklahoma, the fifteen thousand Cherokee still at the removal forts were led out of their compounds for the beginning of what was to be an eight-hundred-mile march. Men, women, and children carried heavy packs over muddy roads and frozen ground. Many walked without shoes. They slept on bare ground with only thin blankets to cover them and no fires to warm them. For nine long months, they endured rain, sleet, and snow, disease, drought, and starvation.

Hundreds of children, as well as adults, died before they reached their allotted lands in Oklahoma. One U.S. Army infantryman recorded the death of twenty-two of his charges in a single night. In all, the diaspora known as the Trail of Tears claimed the lives of more than four thousand Cherokee people, almost one-fourth the total population of that tribe.[a]

---

[a] Patricia Limerick, *The Legacy of Conquest: The Unbroken Past of the American West* (New York: Norton, 1987), 194; Howard Zinn, *A People's History of the United States* (New York: Harper & Row, 1980), 146.

strapped to papoose boards that were hung over the pommel of a saddle or strapped across a mother's shoulders. Toddlers rode in wicker-enclosed travois, while children not much older shared the back of a pony—two or three astride. In crossing swollen rivers, these youngsters were tied on their horses to prevent mishap. Older children rode ponies of their own or sometimes walked. On far-ranging food-gathering trips Apache children always found their place in the rearguard, following in the wake of their elders.[2]

The Great Overland Adventure

Leaving behind relatives, friends, and familiar surroundings, the children who went west with the wagon and handcart trains in the middle of the nineteenth century set out on a six-month, two-thousand-mile trek across prairies, deserts, and mountains, and, except for the babes in arms, many of them walked most of the way. As historian Emmy Werner has noted, these young pioneers endured heat, cold, floods, thirst, and starvation. They suffered from numerous illnesses and accidents, and they saw death come to family members, friends, and strangers. Some of them got lost, some were kidnapped, some were abandoned. In sum, Werner concludes, "The stories of the youngsters on the emigrant trails are a remarkable testimony to the resiliency of the human spirit."[3]

While there is no denying the truth of those words, it is instructive to compare Werner's latter-day assessment of the experience of westering children with comments found in letters, journals, and memoirs of the emigrants themselves. Ruth Moynihan's survey of the adult reminiscences of those who crossed the plains in childhood revealed that most little travelers, in the words of one pioneer, looked upon the "whole affair as one great picnic excursion."[4]

For the children of families that had made successive moves from one home to

Above: *"Thought there was nothing but fun in the journey,"* the caption that ran with this mid-nineteenth-century engraving, espoused the prevailing view of children's attitudes about the westward trek, an attitude also conveyed in many memoirs written by adults who crossed the plains as children.

another before setting out on the longest journey of all, the trip west was little more than business as usual. The Gay children of Greene County, Missouri, were seasoned travelers by the time they left for Oregon in the spring of 1851, the family having already moved from Kentucky to Tennessee to Missouri to Arkansas and then back to Missouri in previous years.[5]

Even for those children with a heritage of mobility, the trip across the plains to the Far West exceeded all other undertakings. "It was a long, long journey, full of grave responsibility to the older members of the family," D. B. Ward admitted in 1913, some sixty years after his overland journey west. "But for me, a lad of fifteen, it was . . . the most interesting six months' period of my life." Thirteen-year-old Martha Edgerton Plassman, who traveled with her family from Ohio to Bannack in present-day Montana in 1863, reported, "There were no regrets on my part at leaving my relatives and my native town. It meant for me adventure."[6]

The adventure began for most children as they assisted their parents in preparing for the journey west. Seven-year-old Benjamin Bonney of Illinois spent several months helping his father build the emigrant wagon that would take him, his parents, and his six brothers and sisters to California in 1845.[7]

Once preparations were completed, the sendoff a family received heightened the excitement of the children: "All the town and part of the county had heard of our departure," Martha Gay Masterson recalled forty-one years after her family left Greene County, Missouri, bound for Oregon Territory. "All places of business and the schools were closed during the forenoon, and everybody came to say goodbye to us. . . . The house and yard and streets were crowded with people. Friends and schoolmates were crying all around us."[8]

Jesse Applegate was seven years old in the spring of 1843 when he set out with great excitement on the journey from St. Clair County, Missouri, to Oregon Territory. That fall, as the family started down the Columbia River on the last leg of their trek, young Jesse's spirit of adventure was undiminished. Having traveled all summer "barefoot through the desert sands, through sagebrush, grease wood, and cactus," he welcomed the ride on the riverboat. Recalling his experience later in life, he admitted that "whirlpools looking like deep basins in the river [and] the lapping, slashing, and rolling of the waves" had alarmed him at first but since "children left to themselves and not alarmed by those they look to for protection, do not borrow trouble, . . .[in due time] the sight of foam and whitecaps ahead occasioned only pleasant anticipation."[9]

In contrast, the memoirs of other emigrant children focus on the discomfort, drudgery, trauma, and losses generated by the journey. The excitement of beginning the journey west was tempered for eight-year-old George Jackson of Hazleton, Iowa, by the grief of having to leave behind a beloved pet. Try as he might, he could not hide his tears that spring morning in 1880 as Jake, his old black cat, walked to the very end of the farmyard fence and then sat there, staring after the wagon that rolled west toward Montana Territory.[10]

Eight-year-old Florence Weeks, traveling from Centreville, Michigan, to California in 1859, was carried across the plains and mountains by her dependable old horse, Muggins, which she described later as "the homeliest piece of horseflesh . . . ever seen—a dirty color, great big head, and crooked hind legs." But homely or no, Florence loved her Muggins and was inconsolable when her parents decided to leave the exhausted horse at the Humboldt Sink, knowing he would never survive the trip over the Sierras.[11]

Despite his initial enthusiasm for the wagon trip west, Benjamin Bonney recalled in adulthood the agony of crossing a sagebrush plain studded with prickly pears: "We children were barefooted and I can remember yet how we limped across the desert, for we cut the soles of our feet on the [spiny needles]."[12]

Children's Chores on the Trail

If the prickly pear needles brought complaints, so too did the seeming drudgery of the chores assigned to children on the trail. One thirteen-year-old walked almost all the way from the Missouri River to the Willamette Valley in Oregon, trailing the family's horses and cattle behind the convoy of wagons, seeing that none were lost and keeping the stragglers from falling too far behind. For ten or twelve miles each day, the girl tramped in the dust stirred up by hundreds of animals and wagons, coming into camp each night with her hair, clothes, skin, mouth, eyes, and ears coated in dust and knowing there would be no water for bathing.[13]

George Jackson started across the country from Iowa bareback on an old mare, herding the family's milk cows but imagining himself a real cowboy headed west. On the Platte River in Nebraska, the Jacksons' train met a group of cowboys trailing cattle from Texas to Omaha. Seeing the little farm boy riding bareback in the rearguard, one of the cowhands offered him a battered old saddle. It was a gift George treasured for a lifetime.[14]

Gathering fuel was another task that often fell to children. In tall-grass prairies where wood was scarce, youngsters were sent out to pull slough grass and twist it into coils for campfire or stove. The job of gathering buffalo dung was considered the perfect assignment for children still full of energy at the end of the day. "Gathering buffalo chips was Ester's [sic] and my job," Florence Weeks wrote in the diary that recorded her family's trip to California. "We were rather finicky about it at first, but found they were as dry as a chip of wood. We had a basket with a handle on each side to carry them."[15]

Jesse Applegate and his friends turned the chore into competitive play, forming teams to conduct the search and then to construct piles of dried manure to be used by their respective families. Nine-year-old Henry Brown, who left his home in Wilmington, Illinois, in the spring of 1847, bound for Oregon in the company of his parents and two younger sisters, also scurried among the dust-covered prickly pear to find fuel for the family campfire each night, then enlisted the help of his seven-year-old sister, Martha Jane, in guarding the family's chips against raids from other children.[16]

Children were also responsible for cooping up the chickens when the train set out in the morning, then letting them out each evening to feed. Boys with hunting dogs and fishing rods were sent out each evening in search of game or fish with which to supplement the standard menu of bacon and salt pork, flapjacks, and dried fruit. Older boys drove wagons and stood watch at night. Andrew Fergus was fourteen when he, his mother, three sisters,

Above: Between 1856 and 1860 many Mormons traveled to Utah in handcart companies like the one depicted in this contemporary engraving. Most of them walked their way west, though the ill and the elderly, infants, and tuckered-out toddlers were frequently nestled among the possessions carried in the carts.

Above: *An emigrant family poses under a sleeping canopy stretched between two wagons. The initial excitement of the journey seems to have dissipated for these children, who have perhaps had their surfeit of "the adventure," with its long, dusty days and thankless chores.*

and a brother-in-law left Little Falls, Minnesota, in 1864 bound for the home his father had established for them in Virginia City, Montana Territory. With a new pony and a borrowed revolver, the boy took his turn as picket against Indian attack.[17]

Boys even younger assumed responsibilities beyond their years. At age eleven, Elisha Brooks and his twin brother lacked both the size and the strength to lift the yoke over the heads of the oxen when they, their mother, an older sister, and three younger brothers left Michigan in 1852 to join their father in California. Yet before their wagon was many miles across the plains, Elisha and his brother had replaced the hired driver at the reins of the family's four-yoke team.[18]

One of the eight oxen who pulled the Brooks family wagon was Old Brock, an animal Elisha had trained from the time he was a calf. As the journey wore on, the Brookses lost four of their oxen to starvation and exhaustion. The last to go down

was Old Nig, Brock's partner. When Brock sank down beside his mate and refused to go on, Elisha carried hay back to him from the family's campsite two miles farther down the trail and waited patiently through a snowstorm until his pet was ready to submit to the yoke once more. The two caught up with the wagon train, and each resumed his duty—Old Brock doing his share to pull the wagon over the Sierras with Elisha at the reins.[19]

As a matter of course, girls helped on the trail with such traditional female chores as caring for children, cooking, sewing, and tending the sick. But some girls also rode horses and drove wagons. Virginia Reed of Springfield, Illinois, crossed the plains in the summer of 1846, traveling most of the time on the back of her beloved pony, Billy. From the Nebraska prairie westward, the thirteen-year-old joined her father and the other men of the company on buffalo hunts.[20]

Sarah Cummins was another girl who was not to be denied the freedom and excitement of the trail. An adolescent when she made the trip, Sarah would "mount [her] riding nag and employ every spare moment in feasting [her] eyes and [her] 'mind's eye.'" She most often rode alone so that she could "halt or proceed at will." In coming upon a stream that was "very treacherous, as to hidden rocks," she would ride into the water, scouting for unseen boulders and advising the oncoming wagons as to the safest route for crossing.[21]

Trailside Diversions

While Sarah Cummins was scouting out the terrain for her company, she was also enjoying the beauty of the western landscape. Children as well as adults wrote about the wildflowers that abounded on the plains in early spring and those that flourished in the mountain passes during the summer months. As the days grew longer, children took walks in the twilight, sometimes climbing a rise or hill to scout the next day's route. When evening chores were done, they played games of tag and rounds of hide-and-seek in the dense sagebrush. They eavesdropped on adult conversation around the campfire, told each other hair-raising stories of Indian assaults, or opened a favorite book.

As much as ten-year-old Mollie Sheehan enjoyed the daytime activities on the trail, she cherished as well those last few moments in the dim light of the evening campfire when she would pull *Uncle Tom's Cabin* or her book of Bible stories from her pack and read—sometimes aloud to her father and mother, sometimes only to herself. A boy not much older than Mollie took *Two Years before the Mast* and Plutarch's *Lives* across the plains with him, and *The Life of Daniel Boone*, *Pilgrim's Progress*, and *Robinson Crusoe* kept other young travelers company.[22]

Many nights the whole company, adults and children alike, enjoyed music and dancing around the campfire as the resident fiddler took over. Mormon emigrants composed a number of hymns and songs to inspire weary travelers, most notably "The Handcart Song":

For some must push, and some must pull
As we go marching up the hill!
So merrily on our way we go,
Until we reach the Valley, O![23]

The Fourth of July was a holiday universally observed by wagon trains as a day of rest and merriment. If the company was on schedule, that holiday was spent in the vicinity of Independence Rock. It was there that the Brooks brothers found the place where their father had carved his name into the rock during his journey west some two years earlier. Rejoicing in their discovery—and in the knowledge that their own journey was half over—the boys gave in to an impulse felt and followed by thousands of children before them and scrambled all the way up the rugged face of the rock.[24]

Graves were often the first landmark children searched for in scouting the terrain af-

ter making camp each night."As soon as we got to camp," Martha Gay Masterson recalled in her memoirs, "We scampered out to see what we could find. . . . If there were any graves near camp we would visit them and read the inscriptions. Sometimes we would see where wolves had dug into the graves after the dead bodies, and we saw long braids of golden hair telling of some young girl's burying place." Masterson and her siblings often saw "human skulls bleached by sun and storms lying scattered around." Though too frightened by the

Above: *Two frontier families pause on a sturdy bridge across a roaring mountain stream, glad to have behind them the countless river crossings made by ford or by ferry during the long journey to Colorado.*

first skulls they saw to even approach them, they soon grew accustomed to them. "We would pick them up and read the verses which some passerby had written on them, then perhaps add a line or two and set them up to attract someone else as they passed by."[25]

While exploring the country around their campsite early one evening, George Jackson and his five-year-old sister, Mercy, found a rough little box on top of a nearby knoll. Inside they discovered the body of a small Indian child who had been buried with her doll and various little playthings. Intrigued, the children brought the doll and a few other "souvenirs" back to camp with them, whereupon they were severely reprimanded by their father and made to "walk clear back and take the things and put them back in the casket where they had found them." It was only in adulthood that the impact of their transgression had its effect on the Jackson siblings; as children, their only regret had been the loss of their booty and that long walk back up the hill.[26]

Births occurred frequently on the trail and were generally occasions for celebration. Early on a morning in mid-June, scant weeks after having begun the trip from Greene County, Missouri, young Martha Gay was awakened by "the wailing of an infant." Instinctively, she turned to her mother to ask whose baby was crying. "Hush," her mother replied, "It is our baby." Martha grew silent at the news, "fearing I might have . . . another brother." The addition of yet another brother to the nine who were her sometime nemeses was more than the thirteen-year-old wanted to contemplate. When she finally got up the courage to ask the fearful question, she was overcome with relief to hear that she had a sister— "surely the cutest and sweetest little sister in all the wide world."[27]

Infants were actually easier to manage on the long journey than were toddlers, since they could be more easily confined and controlled. When they were not sleeping in a nest of blankets within a wagon, small babies were carried by an adult or older sibling, usually across the back in a blanket sling, Indian fashion. Or they could be carried on saddles outfitted with special carryalls. Emergencies prompted ingenuity. In bringing two stranded families out of Death Valley in 1849, John Rogers, the young man who headed the rescue party, "took a long sack and fixed it so that it could be fastened on the ox." Rogers then "cut [a hole] on each side like a pair of saddlebags and a baby was placed in each end. The little fellows would ride thus and sleep half of their time."[28]

Once they had outgrown such contrivances, toddlers were put on their feet. As the trains advanced at the rate of two or three miles an hour, they generally managed to keep up for a while, but when their small legs gave out, they were hoisted to the shoulders of older siblings, parents, or adult friends.

Tragedies on the Trail

A toddler's natural inclination to explore could lead to disaster on the trail. When a three-year-old boy turned up missing soon after the wagon train made camp for the evening, his frantic parents began a search of the surrounding area. It proved futile, and through that long night the company listened helplessly to the howling of the wind and the wolves, fearing the worst. When the wagonmaster decided to move on the next morning, the stricken parents stayed behind to continue what most considered a hopeless search. At midmorning a fellow from another train rode up with the missing boy astride his saddle. He had found the child two miles from the campsite, nearly dead from exposure. Overjoyed, the parents promptly turned their wagon eastward and headed home, having had their surfeit of the great adventure.[29]

Missing children, whatever their age, occasioned great concern among trains heading west. When a young boy who was

Left: *Known as "Exodusters," thousands of blacks fled their sharecropper homes in the Deep South in the late 1870s for the promise of "free ground" and economic and social betterment in Kansas. In this photograph taken on a Mississippi levee, two little girls perch on a crate and chair, waiting with the same hope and determination as their elders for the arrival of a steamboat that may take them to a new life, while their little brother gives in to the boredom of the long wait.*

The Flight to "Free Ground"

What did the end of the trail hold for the children of African American descent who traveled west in the nineteenth century? For Ellen Mason, thirteen years old when she arrived with her mother and two younger sisters in California in 1851, there was hard-won freedom. Brought west from Mississippi in a company of Mormon converts as the slaves of a Robert Smith, Ellen and her sisters walked the entire distance, trailing along in the dust of the caravan beside their mother, Biddy, who was charged with herding Smith's cattle. When Smith, dissatisfied with life in California, a free state, attempted to move his slaves to Texas, Biddy Mason saw her chance and sued for freedom. The district judge of Los Angeles ruled that Biddy and her children were "entitled to their freedom" and could no longer "be held in slavery or involuntary servitude." From Mississippi to Utah to California, the family had walked their way to freedom.[a]

Nearly thirty years after the Masons had established themselves in Los Angeles, a Louisiana sharecropper couple and their four young children made their own bid for a better life. A part of the great "Exoduster" movement, the family of John Solomon Lewis fled their home one spring day in 1879 and for almost three weeks hid in the woods bordering the Mississippi River, waiting for the arrival of a steamer bound for St. Louis,

the gateway to their new home in Kansas. Eventually emboldened by the arrival of other blacks who were also seeking an escape from the terrors of the "nightriders" and the poverty of sharecropping, the Lewis family emerged from the woods to camp on the riverbank until the *Grand Tower*, the "government boat," took them aboard.

While many other Exodusters suffered exposure and starvation while waiting on the riverbanks for steamboats that refused to stop for them, the Lewis family arrived safely in St. Louis, where they hailed another steamer that took them up the Missouri to the open prairie of Kansas. Having survived the uncertainties of a two-month trip from a sharecropper's cabin in Louisiana to their homestead in Kansas, the four Lewis children joined hands with their parents and in a drenching rain gave thanks for the "free ground" upon which they stood.[b]

---

[a] JoAnn Levy, *They Saw the Elephant: Women in the California Gold Rush* (Norman: University of Oklahoma Press, 1992) 214–15; William Katz, *The Black West*, (Garden City, N.Y.: Doubleday, 1971), 129.

[b] Painter, *Exodusters*, 3–4, 186.

Above: A miner's family poses beside the dogsled that carried their belongings across the Chilkoot Pass to the Klondike goldfields in the early years of the twentieth century. Families trekking to the last frontier were far more limited in what they could take with them than were those who had crossed the plains by wagon a half-century before. While most children of earlier pioneers were, by now, living in or near thriving settlements, children bound for the Yukon would find nothing but a rough gold camp at the end of their trail.

driving one of his family's wagons unaccountably took a wrong turn where a canyon divided the trail through Death Valley, the entire company pulled to a halt, despite their eagerness to have the desert behind them. Fortunately, the boy discovered his own mistake before having gone too far, and he was retracing his route and "whistling in absolute unconcern" by the time his parents, who had been following his wagon tracks in the sand, came across him.[30]

Children who fell ill on the trail prompted as much worry for a parent as did those who wandered off. Elisha Brooks retained vivid memories of himself and his five siblings "all lying in a row on the ground in our tent, somewhere in Iowa, stricken with the measles, while six inches of snow covered all the ground and the trees were brilliant with icicles."[31] There were more serious illnesses to cope with: Cholera was

a constant threat in emigrant companies, and children fell victim to fevers, dysentery, smallpox, and scurvy.

All travelers were on constant guard against accidents with wagons, but there was no train that did not have its share of mishaps, some more serious than others. Like other children in her train, ten-year-old Catherine Sager soon grew skilled at leaping out of the moving wagon, although she had been warned more than once not to do so. One day the hem of her dress caught on an axe handle as she leapt, and she fell under the rolling wheels. Her left leg was badly crushed before her father could stop the oxen, and she was in agonizing pain for weeks. Though she survived her 1844 journey to Oregon, the accident left her crippled for life.[32]

An eight-year-old traveling in the train ahead of Henry Brown and his family "fell from the tung [of the family wagon]," according to one witness, and "the wheels run over him and mashed his head and kil[led] him stone dead he never moved." Young Brown himself witnessed the funeral that night. It was a "strange sight," he recalled. "The people stood around . . . as they consigned [the boy] to rest with a boot box for a coffin."[33]

This was not the only funeral young Brown witnessed in the course of his journey west. Within a month of leaving Illinois, Henry's father had contracted a fever that proved fatal. He was buried at daybreak the morning after his death in a grave dug eight feet deep, lined with a few boards, and covered with rock. As a precaution against raids by wolves and grave robbers, the train's forty wagons were then driven over his resting place, the depression made by the passing wheels was filled with more dirt, and the wagons circled and rolled over the spot one final time, erasing any evidence of the grave's existence. The slow, sad ritual only accentuated young Henry's grief at the loss of his father.[34]

Only weeks after having begun their journey west with high hopes, the parents of twelve-year-old John Hoover buried their son on the banks of the Platte beneath a crude marker on which they had carved, "Died, June 18. 49. . . . Rest in peace, sweet boy, for thy travels are over." At the turnoff for the Lassen Trail in the Sierra Nevadas, not far from what should have been her new home, another child was buried by grieving parents. Over her small grave they left an unadorned inscription: "Mary Jane McClelland, departed this life, Aug. 18th, 1849, aged 3 yrs. 4 mos." A pine board at the head of one trailside grave bore the inscription "Two children, killed by a stampede."[35]

J. Goldsborough Bruff, the captain of a mining company traveling overland to the California goldfields, reported a heart-wrenching scene in a winter camp in the Sierras, where he found a four-year-old boy in desperate straits. Apparently, the boy's father— "an inhuman wretch" from St.

Louis—had forcibly taken little Billy from his mother and headed west in the company of another woman. The boy had been "treated in the most brutal manner" ever since, and on that cold night in mid-November when Bruff first saw him, he was lying on damp blankets "and endeavoring to pull a wet buffalo robe over him, but it was too heavy for his feeble strength." When Bruff asked the father's permission to take the child into his tent for treatment, the man cavalierly consented—then promptly packed up and left camp.

Clearly, the boy had been physically abused. "He is pale, very weak, complains of pains, and [bleeds] at the nose and ears," Bruff wrote. One night when the child complained of hunger and there was noth-

Above: The solitary grave marker of four-year-old Elva Ingram, who died on the Oregon Trail far from her Iowa home, is a graphic reminder of the tragedies some families faced on a journey that had invariably begun with great excitement and high hopes.

Above: *A snow camp in the High Sierras.*

In the depths of the winter of 1846–47, tragedy struck a group of emigrants attempting to cross from present-day Reno, Nevada, to Sacramento, California, by way of the mountain pass that now bears their party's name. Thirty-five members of the group, fifteen of them children, died when the Donner party was trapped in that camp in the High Sierras.

Patty Reed and Nancy Graves were both eight years old when their families joined the company of some eighty emigrants—nine families in all—that left Springfield, Illinois, in mid-April 1846 under the leadership of brothers George and Jacob Donner, prosperous farmers in search of better land. Already far behind schedule, the party was camped at Truckee Lake on October 31 when the first heavy snow of the season struck the mountains. The weather never let up thereafter, and six weeks later the party remained trapped under deep snow, huddled "in dark little cabins" and in tents made of canvas, quilts, and buffalo robes. They had killed and eaten most of their cattle; they had boiled the hides and chewed on them. In desperation, Patty Reed's family had even killed their dog, eating "his head and feet & hide & evry thing about him." Other families killed and ate the mice that ran through the camp.

Shortly before Christmas, realizing that their situation was growing worse with each passing day, Nancy Graves's father fashioned fifteen pairs of snowshoes, packed provisions enough to last six days, and started across the pass with fourteen others—including three children. More than a month later, the group finally reached the safety of the Johnson Ranch, though in the interim, eight of them had died, among them Lemuel Murphy, a twelve-year-old whose body was cannibalized by the starving survivors.

Back at the camp, as January turned to February with no sign of a rescue party, death became a daily occurrence. Even so, the Reed family never lost hope. Patty's thirteen-year-old half-sister, Virginia, later described "the long sleepless nights, the cold dark days . . . passed in that little Cabin under the snow." Ironically, there were "pleasant hours" too. "We used to sit and talk together and some times almost forget oneself for a while," Virginia recalled. The family also had a few books that she and Patty read "over and over."

On February 18, two months after the snowshoe party had first set out, a rescue team of seven men arrived at the camp with provisions; five days later, they started back across the mountains with twenty-three people from the party, sixteen of them children, ages eighteen to one. Among those who began the trek were Patty and Virginia Reed, their mother, and two of their brothers. Patty's friend, Nancy Graves, who was not strong enough to attempt the crossing, was left behind with her mother, but three of Nancy's six brothers and sisters began the trek out.

Before the party had progressed very far, it was obvious that neither Patty Reed nor her three-year-old brother, Tommy, had the strength to make the trip and both must be escorted back to their makeshift

the Donner Party

winter cabin. Virginia was heart-broken, but Patty was stoical. "Well, Ma," she said to her mother as she was led back up the trail, "if you never see me again do the best you can."

"I think my little brother James was the smallest child that walked across," Virginia Reed reported. "Poor little fellow, he would have to place his knee on the hill of snow between each step of the snowshoes and climb over. . . . We were . . . very much afraid that he would give out. . . . [W]e kept telling him that every step he took he was gitting nearer Papa." One man told the five-year-old that he would "buy him a horse in Cal[ifornia] , and he would not have to walk any more." With such assurances, James survived the trek and with the others reached the Johnson Ranch within ten days of having struck out through the deep snow.

It was early March before a second relief party reached the High Sierras and started back with seventeen persons, including fourteen children. Patty and Tommy Reed were among them, as were Nancy Graves, three of her siblings, and her mother. Three days out, the party was waylaid by yet another fierce storm. When the weather cleared, the leaders pressed on with the strongest of the company, but Nancy Graves was left behind with her mother, her siblings, and eight others. That night, as they sat around the fire pit, Mrs. Graves and her young son Franklin died. Soon thereafter, they were eaten by their starving companions—including eight-year-old Nancy, who would be haunted by that dark incident for the rest of her life.

While Nancy Graves huddled by the fire in the mountains, Patty and Tommy Reed marched on toward the Johnson Ranch.

Patty was carried the last few miles by her father, who had led the second rescue attempt. Eventually, Nancy Graves, her father, and two of her siblings also reached safety.

In all, fourteen of the forty-one children of the Donner party died in the mountains, and the infant Elizabeth Graves died shortly after arriving at Sutter's Fort. More than half the twenty-six surviving children were orphaned by the tragedy.[a]

-----

[a] Werner, *Pioneer Children on the Journey West*, 36–52.

Left: *This tiny four-inch doll belonged to eight-year-old Patty Reed, who carried her out of the Sierras in March 1847 after having been stranded for over four months with other members of the Donner Party—an ordeal that claimed the lives of fifteen children and twenty adults.*

ing to feed him, Bruff diverted his attention by giving him "a spool of cotton to play with and while unwinding it, he seemed to be reminded of his home, of his mother . . . saying 'Mother's cotton, Mother's scissors, Mother has bread, and Mother has cake, and Mother has tea.'"

"Poor little creature!" Bruff scribbled on New Year's Day, 1850. "We done all we could for the poor little sufferer, but by 11 a.m. he was extricated from all the hardships of life. . . . I procured a piece of white cotton, stripped the boy, washing him with snow, and tied him up in the cloth, and secured the tent to prevent the wolves carrying him off." The next day, Bruff buried the small body, piling stones on the grave and hewing a headboard on which he inscribed,

WILLIAM
Infant son of
LAMBKIN
an Unnatural Father,
Died Jan. 1, 1850[36]

Native children sometimes fared as poorly as did Billy Lambkin. Just outside an emigrant encampment near a large lake in northern California, a picket found an Indian girl about eight years old huddled against the mountain cold not far from the site of a recent Indian battle. Benjamin Bonney of Illinois, who was about the same age as the little girl, later recalled that she "was perfectly naked, her long black hair was matted, and she was covered with scars from head to feet. . . . she was suffering from hunger and . . . the flies had almost eaten her up. . . . She had apparently crept [away from the battle] . . . and had been left [behind]."

Divided as to what to do with the child, the emigrant party voted to leave her where they had found her, though Bonney's mother, his aunt, and a few others who had opposed the decision "stayed behind to do all they could do for her." The child's agony was so great, however, that eventually one of the young men who

had stayed to help was so overwhelmed by the hopelessness of her condition that he "put a bullet through her head and put her out of her misery."[37]

Encounters with Indians

Despite the fact that fewer than one-tenth of all wagon trains reported any sort of hostile act by Native Americans and most children crossed the plains without ever seeing an Indian, reports of isolated incidents kept the possibility of an attack uppermost in the emigrant mind.[38]

"My greatest fear was Indians," Martha Gay Masterson wrote in her reminiscences of her overland journey of 1851. When rumors of hostile Indians in the vicinity reached the company with which the Gay family was traveling, Masterson recalled that "there was little thought of sleeping [that night] except by little children and innocent babes." With the coming of light, Martha and her older sister, Mamie, were aghast to find two arrows piercing the wagon cover above their heads, but relieved to discover that their train had suffered no other damage.[39]

In an ambush in eastern Wyoming a young boy was captured by an Indian band, then traded to some passing emigrants several days later in exchange for a horse. When those emigrants eventually caught up with the wagon train that had taken in his mother and five-year-old sister following the ambush, the boy was finally restored to his family.[40]

Elisha Brooks and his family had more encounters with Indians than did most emigrants. Experiencing numerous troubles with their wagon—which meant that they were more than once left behind by whatever train they happened to be traveling with—the stranded family was once assisted by a migrating band of Crows who fell in beside them and kept them company for a week. Years later, Elisha could still see the "old ox team with six wild, ragged children and a woman once called white" who straggled along behind their "colorfully dressed, well provisioned, and peaceful" Indian escort.[41]

Elisha's experience with the Crow stood in stark contrast to his earlier experience with the Sioux. Just after leaving Fort Laramie, the train with which his family was traveling met a party of Sioux, one hundred men strong, lining both sides of the trail. The wagonmaster, counting on the proximity of the fort to keep the Indians at bay, decided to drive on through the gauntlet. Eleven-year-old Elisha, who was at the reins of the family's wagon, kept his fears and his team well in check until one of the Indians cracked a whip over the back of Old Brock, his pet ox. "I sprang with a scream and snatched the whip out of the Indian's hands before he could strike another blow," Brooks recalled, "for we never whipped Old Brock. . . . and the Whites and the Reds began to swarm."[42]

The incident ended without serious consequences, but it was not the last brush Elisha was to have with that group of Sioux. When his mother bought a pony from one of the Indians, Elisha leapt aboard the mustang and was straightaway carried, "clinging for his life," back to the nearby Sioux encampment. Certain that he would be taken captive—or worse—Elisha slid from his mount as the Sioux, quickly recovering from their momentary shock at seeing a white boy gallop into camp astride one of their horses, began to dance around him. Only when the dance turned into a celebratory feast—to which he was invited—did Elisha regain his courage. At the conclusion of the festivities, the Indians escorted the boy back to his train, much to the relief of his anxious mother.[43]

Many emigrant children were more intrigued by than fearful of Indians. Thirteen-year-old Virginia Reed, who crossed the plains in 1846 with the Donner party, often encountered war parties of Sioux when she was on buffalo hunts with her father and other company members. "They are fine-looking Indians," she reported,

A Different Perspective

"I was a small child when the first white people came into our country," Sarah Winnemucca wrote in her autobiography, *Life among the Piutes*. "My people were scattered at that time over nearly all the territory now known as Nevada." Little Thocme-tony, or Shell Flower, as Winnemucca was known in girlhood, heard how her maternal grandfather, a leader among the Northern Paiute people, had responded to the arrival of strangers who "had hair on their faces, and were white." "My white brothers," he had said, "my long-looked-for white brothers have come at last!"

Within a very short time, however, the Paiute leader's perception of his "white brothers" was radically changed by the behavior of the settlers and soldiers. "[T]here was a great excitement among my people on account of fearful news coming from different tribes," Winnemucca recalled in adulthood. "Our mothers told us that the whites were killing everybody."[a]

Two decades after Winnemucca's experience, Ohiyesa, a young Sioux growing up on the plains of the Dakotas, first came in contact with white people. "I had heard marvelous things of this people," he recalled in a turn-of-the-century autobiography written under his anglicized name, Charles Eastman. "In some things we despised them, in others we regarded them as *wakan* (mysterious), a race whose power bordered upon the supernatural." When as a boy, Eastman first heard that the whites had a "fire-boat," he could not understand "how they could unite two elements which cannot exist together. I thought the water would put out the fire, and the fire would consume the boat if it had the shadow of a chance. This was to me a preposterous thing!" Incredulity turned to fear as he heard that "the Big Knives" had created a "fire-boat-walks-on-mountains," and he was understandably relieved to discover that the movement of this "fire-boat-walks-on-mountains" was restricted to the path followed by the tracks upon which it glided and could not, after all, chase and devour an Indian child.[b]

---

[a] Werner, *Pioneer Children on the Journey West*, 22.
[b] Jay David, ed., *The American Indian: The First Victim* (New York: William Morrow, 1972), 108–109.

Above: A large Mormon train circles for the evening at a way station just east of Echo Canyon in Utah, their journey almost done. The clouds of dust are not yet settled, the animals not yet tended, the wagon in the foreground not yet repaired, but one more day's travel is behind them.

"and I was not the least afraid of them. . . . They never showed any inclination to disturb us." She enjoyed watching the warriors react to their own images in the mirror she offered them. "Whenever they came near trying to get a peep at their war-paint and feathers I would raise the glass and laugh," she recalled. There is, of course, no way to turn the mirror around to know the thoughts of the Sioux as they beheld the "Pioneer Palace car," the two-story wagon in which Virginia Reed crossed the Nebraska plains.[44]

The Resilience of Youth

The overland journey called for patience and resolution, qualities not often exhibited by children under ordinary circumstances, but qualities displayed in abundance on the trail. Staunch supporters of their mother's decision to brave the trip west in order to join their father in California, the six Brooks children, ages thirteen to three, were the ones who kept her spirits up when the difficulties of the trip and her sense of "loneliness and utter helplessness" led her to question the wisdom of going on. "For a moment she appeared to lean on [us]," Elisha Brooks recalled in his memoirs. "She asked us if we wanted to go on, and if we thought we could drive the team, and if we were afraid of the Indians. Of course we could drive the team, and we had just lost our fear of Indians; besides, were we not almost there?"[45]

J. Goldsborough Bruff, the mining company captain who befriended Billy Lambkin, recorded the endurance of two small travelers who were accompanying their father and a pair of lame oxen on the Lassen Trail along the Feather River in the High Sierras. "The little fellow," Bruff wrote, was "blinking back his tears, stumbling with weariness; his sister hovering beside him, exhorting, cajoling . . ., 'Never mind, Buddy, taint far to grass and water.'"[46]

One pair of travelers on the Lassen Trail across the Sierras happened upon a woman and her three small children. The little ones were carrying packs almost as large and heavy as themselves, the bags being "made of shirts, the lower part tied into a bag shape with a string, the sleeves securing the burden to the little bearer's body." When a tree toppled by high winds killed both her husband and her son, the woman had prepared her three surviving children to continue the journey, by giving them as many provisions as they could carry in the hastily devised packs. Seeing that the children were struggling with their burdens

and that the woman herself was exhausted and frightened, the two men invited the woman to join them on the trail until they should meet a train that would take her in.[47]

Trail's End

For some children, such experiences as these ended any sense of the journey as one "great picnic excursion." The death of his father on the plains moved nine-year-old Henry Brown from childhood to adulthood almost overnight. While the early weeks on the trail had been full of such childish diversions as stealing the buffalo chips collected by friends, the weeks after his father's death were a blur of weariness, cold, heat, acrid dust, alkali water, mosquitoes, and perilous ascents and descents. In the Oregon foothills the road became a nightmare, a quagmire trapping dead and dying oxen. For Henry Brown there seemed to be no end to the journey he had undertaken in such high spirits just months before.[48]

For eight-year-old Homer Thomas of Illinois, the end of the trail brought little to repay him for the discomforts and drudgery of the journey. "On the Platte, the musquitoes half eat us up, & it was hot as fire, & mighty dusty," he wrote his grandmother from Montana Territory. "I am mighty glad you didn't come with us, you could not [have] stood it, for it was mighty hard for me to stand. If I had known what this kind of a country and so long a road it was, I bet you I never would have come out here to see Virginia City."[49]

Other children reached the end of the trail with spirits undimmed and the sense of adventure still intact. Seven-year-old Benjamin Bonney camped with his parents and six siblings at the foot of the Sierras in 1845 near a "beautiful, ice-cold, crystal-clear mountain stream." It was October, and the water in the stream was low, exposing many sand and gravel bars. On one of these gravel bars Bonney saw what he thought was a grain of wheat, but upon picking up the pea-sized object he found it surprisingly heavy. Taking it into camp, he sought out one of the company's elders. Dr. Gildea knew immediately what the boy had found, yet cautioned Benjamin's father not to talk of it until they could return the next spring and confirm the discovery.

But it was not to be. Dr. Gildea, along with Benjamin's oldest brother and a sister, succumbed to "mountain fever" that winter, and those deaths meant an end to the dream of returning to the camp in the foothills. Three years later gold was discovered

Above: Long after this family had established a homestead in Johnson County, Kansas, the wagon that carried them west remained the family conveyance.

at Sutter's Mill not far from Benjamin's stream, but by then the boy and his family had moved on to Oregon.[50]

Like the Bonneys, many of the families who crossed the plains continued to move from settlement to settlement or homestead to homestead or mining camp to mining camp, the "fartherest fields" always seeming to be the greenest—or the most golden. Little Jessie Dillon was two years old when her parents left Virginia in 1862, eager for a new life in the West. Reaching eastern Oregon, the little family settled first in the mining camp of Auburn. A year later they were in the Boise Basin, and within another year they were in The

Dalles. And then in Portland. By the time Jessie was six years old, she had lived in five different settlements—and had no doubt played with many other frontier children for whom serial migration was a way of life.[51]

Water Routes West

Not all emigrants reached their destinations in the West by crossing the plains in a prairie schooner. In the middle of the nineteenth century hundreds of families from the East Coast, Midwest, and Southeast made their way to various eastern and southern port cities to board packets that carried them around the Horn to San

MONTANA GOLD MINES.

FOR FORT BENTON,

AND

Fort Union,
Virginia City,
Bannack City,
Silver Creek,
Deer Lodge City,

AND

Deer Lodge Diggings,
Prickly Pear,
Last Chance,
Gallatin and Bosman.

THE NEW, VERY FAST AND LIGHT DRAUGHT

STEAMER LUELLA,

H. K. HAZLETT, Master.

Built expressly for the Upper Missouri, will leave as above,

on *Wednesday April 17* at *12* o'clock, P. M.
1867

For Freight or Passage, apply to

JOHNSTON'S PRINT, PITTSBURGH.

Left: Not all westering children crossed the plains in ox-drawn wagons. Some, whose elders were enticed by ads such as this 1867 hand-bill for the Missouri River steamer Luella, took the water route from St. Louis to the river's westernmost port, Fort Benton, Montana Territory. Though less reliable than travel by wagon train, riverboat travel was less expensive. And it was faster. If the river stayed high and Indians did not waylay the boat, the journey from Missouri took two and a half months or less.

Francisco, a voyage that could take up to seven months. Some travelers opted to sail south only as far as Panama or Nicaragua, where they crossed the isthmus to the Pacific and continued by ship to San Francisco, a journey that could be accomplished in little more than a month, given the right conditions.

It was by the latter route that six-year-old George Stearns went west from New Hampshire with his parents and infant brother in 1853. Oblivious to the discomforts experienced by his mother, who crossed Nicaragua on muleback with a four-month-old baby in her arms, young George rode proudly along on the mule in front of her, too fascinated by the jungle scenes that surrounded him to share his parents' anxiety over rumors of illness in the Pacific port ahead. Though five of their fellow passengers died of yellow fever on the steamer that carried the Stearns family from San Juan del Sur to San Francisco, George, his parents, and his baby brother all arrived at their destination in good health.[52]

Some families chose the Missouri River route to the frontier. The five Levengood children and their mother set out by rail from Covington, Kentucky, in the spring of 1867, bound for reunion with their father, who had preceded them to Montana Territory some three years earlier. Boarding a stern-wheeler in St. Louis, they steamed their way up the Missouri. Although somewhat less expensive than overland travel, river travel was also less reliable. The upper reaches of the Missouri were shallow, and gigantic snags concealed beneath the water were capable of piercing the hull of any vessel—even 150-ton steamers. Those upper reaches were also controlled by hostile Indians who found the slow-moving boats an easy target.[53]

Even so, the Levengoods found safe passage. Debarking at Fort Benton, three-year-old Carlos Levengood was understandably wary of the bewhiskered stranger who met them there, but he was soon chattering away to the father who had left home before his birth, telling him all about the Indians he had seen camped along the banks of the river, about the strong men who had leapt from the boat to pull it through the shallows, and about the hat he had lost overboard sometime on the trip west.[54]

Myer Newmark was fourteen years old in mid-December of 1852 when he boarded the *Carrington*, a large, graceful clipper ship, and set sail from New York harbor. With his mother, little brother, and four sisters, he was bound for reunion with his father, who had preceded the family to San Francisco a year earlier. Myer's diary of his four-month voyage, which he titled "Ship's Log around the Horn," provides a richly detailed account of the journey. Excerpts appear below.

THURSDAY, DECEMBER 16TH   We sailed at 8 o'clock a.m., Uncle John escorted us as far as the tow boat went, . . . and then we were left to our reflections to travel for sixteen thousand miles. In the afternoon . . . our whole party set to and cast up our accounts [vomited]. Caroline [Myer's seven-year-old sister] commenced, and I was the worst of the lot; however, we continued to sail brightly along.

FRIDAY, DECEMBER 17TH   A great storm arose against us about the middle of the day, and we covered the blankets over us glad to get into our berths. . . . The sea was mountains high, and two life-boats attached to each side of our ship [were] carried off, together with a large portion of fresh stores and, worst of all, our Christmas turkey.

FRIDAY, DECEMBER 24TH   The wind shifted around, but it is still in our favor and in this short space of time we have run 1800 miles from New York. The weather is delightful and the beautiful moonlight nights we spend on deck are really sublime. We are all in fine spirits and pass our time very happily. . . . [T]he only thing we miss is the milk.

SATURDAY, DECEMBER 25TH, Christmas Day   It is a beautiful day . . . . The sea and the sky are a most beautiful blue, and everything looks happy, merry and cheerful. We all did justice to the dainty dinner set before us, which consisted of roast & boiled fowl, vegetables, plum pudding and apple sauce, fruits & cider. [The Newmarks were Jews who kept the Sabbath during their voyage, though they obviously participated in the spirit of the Christian holiday as well.]

MONDAY, DECEMBER 27TH   The wind is high and [we] are going at a great rate. This morning we had a good ducking on deck from a spray which covered us. The children were very cross, particularly Edward [Myer's three-year-old brother] so much so that we threatened to put him in the hole.

SATURDAY, JANUARY 1ST, 1853 . . . Dear Mamma cut up our New Years cake and gave all hands on board a piece with a glass of Port wine. . . . We are now 4000 miles from New York.

FRIDAY, JANUARY 7TH   There is no alteration in the wind or weather and if it continues so till tomorrow evening, we may be on the line [the equator]. The Captain says it is one of the quickest runs he ever made, five thousand miles in twenty-three days; it is near one third of our journey. We live first rate, this morning we had buckwheat cakes for breakfast and pea soup and fowls for dinner; . . . after breakfast the children are dressed and go on deck. Mamma and Matilda [Myer's sixteen-year-old sister] sew till it is time for dinner, previous to which we put the two young ones to bed, who as you may suppose, are the whole time squalling. . . .[I]f it was not for those two we would spend a very plesant time.

WEDNESDAY, JANUARY 12TH   A good steady breeze still continues to carry us toward Cape Horn. . . . [W]e came up to [a ship] at twelve o'clock today. . . . Before seeing her closely, we knew her to be English, as she hoisted her flag while with delight we unfurled the pride of the world—the Stars & Stripes. . . . [W]e left her in the shade and at four oclock . . .we were 6 miles ahead of her, across the line, a good steady breeze. . ., plenty to eat and . . . we are all very well satisfied.

THURSDAY, JANUARY 20TH . . . I pass my time in reading and taking care of Edward. I have been reading Percival Keene, David Copperfield by Dickens. I am trying to learn Caroline reading and writing and Sarah [his eleven-year-old sister] Hebrew.

THURSDAY, JANUARY 27TH   It is very rough indeed and the wind is dead ahead . . . . Though the ship rocks very much and everything is topsy turvy, we all keep our health, though dear Mamma feels very squeamish.

Log around the Horn"

FRIDAY, FEBRUARY 11TH . . . The weather is beautiful this morning and about 11 o'clock we saw a penguin. They are only seen in the vicinity of Cape Horn. We cannot be a great way from it. We have been 56 days out.

FRIDAY, FEBRUARY 18TH . . . We are now at the extreme point of Cape Horn and the weather is cold, stormy and disagreeable. We all wish ourselves in San Francisco, California.

THURSDAY, MARCH 24TH . . . Yesterday the Captain presented dear Mamma a drawing of the "Carrington" in full sail, beautifully executed by himself. We are now about five degrees from the line. I trust that . . . three weeks hence, we shall be with dear Father.

FRIDAY, APRIL 1ST   Today being All Fools Day . . . Mr. Ellery, our mate, made a hollow tube in imitation of a flute and told me to blow it in Miss Palmer's ears as hard as I could. Of course, [I did] it thinking it was to make a fool of her, instead of which I got my face filled with powder.

TUESDAY, APRIL 19TH   This morning the whole of the main land is clearly seen together with Point [Reyes], which is exactly 37 miles from the town of San Francisco, but there is no wind and we are not likely to get in to day.

WEDNESDAY, APRIL 20TH, 1853   At two o'clock this morning while we were yet asleep dear Mama heard the pilot call "Port." Of course, she was up in a minute and called us. We dressed ourselves and waited till morning, when at ten o'clock dear father . . . came out in a boat. Then you can easily imagine our feelings. We then went in a little boat ashore. Once more on land my task is done. Trusting you will excuse all imperfections, allow me to subscribe myself.   Yours very truly, Myer J. Newmark [a]

———

[a] The original diary exists as Manuscript 725 in the Southwest Museum, Los Angeles, California. A transcript was published under the title "The Journey around the Horn," in *Western States Jewish Historical Quarterly* (now *Western States Jewish History*) 2, no. 4 (July 1970), 227–345.

Westward by Rail

"At the start the cars are rude but cleanly. Plenty of fresh water is provided. Some effort is made, too, to keep the air fresh and the car decent, but this is very difficult. Most of the passengers are little accustomed to ventilation or to cleanly habits. Pipes are lighted, meals are spread in which sausage, cheese, garlic, and sourkrout form prominent elements, and their mingled odors combine with the smoke of cheap tobacco to render the cars insupportable. Then there are children, and sometimes sick ones; . . . When the train stops, laden with its miscellaneous freight, the adults are glad to alight, the children rush eagerly about gathering the oddest mementos of their journey. Bits of wood and iron, stones, oyster shells, and stray twigs [or] leaves, particularly if it be autumn, are proudly distributed about the cars. Occasionally a kitten is captured to the delight of the whole carload. Until it manages to escape, it is petted, fed, put to sleep in the dinner pails, locked in the arms of its friends, and rarely abused."[a]

———

[a] *Harper's Weekly*, February 10, 1883, 86.

A Rail Journey West

Almost twenty years after the five Levengood children met their father on the dock at Fort Benton, six little Christies—five boys, the oldest nine years of age, and baby Eliza—were ushered by their mother onto a Northern Pacific railcar at St. Paul, Minnesota. The children were full of excitement for they were on their way to join their father on their new homestead in Montana Territory. Two days later, they spilled out of the train and onto the platform in Bozeman, advancing on their waiting father from all sides. "Such a host of little chaps with rolls of Blankets and valises and Baskets and all saying at once oh here is pa," David Christie, the proud father, wrote home to Minnesota the next day. The little family had "got through first rate [with] plenty of lunch and Didies," he assured his folks back on the farm.[55]

A Very Different Journey

The sense of family adventure that surrounded the Christie children's train trip to their new home in the West stands in stark contrast to the despair experienced by hundreds of young Chinese girls trapped in the Asiatic "slave trade" that began in the early 1850s. Lai Chow was only twelve years old when she was "bought" from her family in China and smuggled with two dozen other young girls in crates marked "dishware" on a vessel bound for San Francisco, there to be pressed into a life of prostitution.[56] Though the details of her journey are lost to history, one can sense the horror of that passage.

Not all young Chinese girls who came to "the Golden Mountain" without their families came as victims of the slave trade. Mary Tape crossed the Pacific as an eleven-year-old in the company of missionaries. Though her passage was a far less traumatic experience than was Lai Chow's, Mary still knew the homesickness and fear that came from being taken from her home and handed over to a family that had no understanding of her language or her culture.[57]

The half million children who made the journey west in the middle to late years of the nineteenth century came from different directions and under different circumstances. They came bearing dreams passed on to them by parents who had little or no regard for the fact that the achievement of their goals meant the disruption of the lives of the Native American and Hispanic families for whom the region had long been home. At journey's end, finding themselves in surroundings quite different from what they had known and, in many cases, from what they had expected, these frontier children explored their new environment and, with their families, set about the business of establishing a home in the West.

Above: Chinese children newly arrived at the Angel Island (San Francisco) immigration center, ca. 1915. The strangeness of her first experience of America shows in the expression of the younger girl, while her sister seems ready to meet the new world.

Opposite: Rail travel west was shown in all of its color and complexities in this engraving from the February 10, 1883, Harper's Weekly. The inset contains extracts from the article that accompanied the illustration. The writer described the train's occupants as mostly immigrants freshly arrived from Europe and on their way "inland."

Homes and Habitats

Frontier Children and Their Environment

To the children of emigrant families, the rugged landscape of the trans-Mississippi West could seem strange and somewhat foreboding. Climate and terrain, as well as vegetation and wildlife, were generally quite different from what these children had known "back home," and they reacted with a mixture of wonder and woe to the parching heat of the treeless prairies, the gloom of the redwood forests, the craggy heights of the Rockies and the Sierras. But for the children of the Sioux and the Kansa, the Navajo and the Apache, the Mohave and the Cayuse, there was nothing foreign or forbidding in the vast plains, the barren desertlands, and the isolated coastal valleys they called home.

At Home with the Landscape

To young Jumping Badger—remembered today as Sitting Bull, powerful leader of the Lakota Sioux—the grassy plains of the upper Missouri in the 1840s teemed with the good things of life. With his people, he roamed the plains, following the game in the warmer seasons and retiring to sheltered valleys with the onset of winter. The tipi, that highly portable conical skin tent, was his home year-round. In winter months the tipi was warmed by a fire built at the center of the enclosure, its smoke drawn off by wind flaps at the top of the cone, and over this same fire the family meals were prepared. In summer the cooking fire was built outside the tipi and the buffalo hides were released from their pegs and rolled up a short distance from the ground to allow circulation of cooling breezes.

The boy, his parents, and his two sisters slept on thick hides laid on the floor at the sides of the tipi. Backrests, the dwelling's only other furnishings, were placed on the ground at the wall opposite its entrance; there his father, who was chief of the Hunkpapa, talked and smoked with his visitors. The foods consumed by the boy's people were those most easily obtained from the land on which they camped. Fresh and dried buffalo and antelope meat and berries were the meals to which his mother called him.[1]

For his cousins to the East, the children of the Dakota Sioux, home through most of the year was an earthen lodge, a low, wood-framed building covered with earth and bark or thatched grass. Some of these

Opposite: Three children and their dog and burro pose outside a store whose multilingual advertisements attest to the cosmopolitan nature of mining towns in the frontier West.

Left: Children of Northern Cheyenne chief Two Moon sit with their mother outside the family's lodge on the Lame Deer Agency in southeastern Montana. Although reduced to reservation living by the time this photo was taken in 1896, the Cheyenne still maintained many elements of their previous way of life—note the tipi, the tipi frame, and strips of meat drying on the pole—while incorporating such aspects of the Anglo world as iron pots, tin pans and buckets, and china plates.

Above: An artist's early 1800s engraving of a Mandan village on the upper Missouri in present-day North Dakota. Children growing up in this well-established settlement lived in large lodges made of earth reinforced with bark and thatched grass and housing several families.

Right: Women and children of a nomadic Shoshone people, the Sheepeaters, outside a wickiup. Members of this tribe lived in tipis and wickiups in the arid regions of Wyoming, following the bighorn sheep, living without horses, and depending upon the bow and arrow until late in the nineteenth century.

lodges were large enough to accommodate several families and all their possessions; others were designed to house a single family. Beds of buffalo robes lined some of the walls, and raised platforms used for eating and for storing food, utensils, tools, and weapons lined the others. One area of the lodge was dedicated as a sacred place for prayer. Far less nomadic than the Lakota, the Dakota Sioux cultivated corn and squash, and these vegetables, along with nuts and berries, rounded out a diet based on the meat of the animals they hunted.[2]

Far to the south, in Arizona, young Maria Chona, a Papago, lived with her family in a hut made of woven grasses. Prickly pear cactus and cultivated corn were dietary staples for Maria's people. Each year when the cactus dried up and the corn had been harvested, the Papago moved to their winter huts in Mexico to await the coming of spring and their return to the hill country of Arizona.[3]

On the coast of Oregon Territory, the children of the Tillamook lived year-round in fishing villages, small clusters of huts made of cedar taken from their vast forests. Like earth lodges, these houses could accommodate several families. Sleeping and eating platforms lined the walls, while the floor was sometimes covered with layers of matted ferns and rushes. The diet of the Tillamook child was highly dependent on fish (especially salmon and halibut) wild game, and roots.[4]

Whether on the plains, in the dry, arid Southwest, or along the Pacific coast, Indian children moved easily in their environment. To outside observers, they seemed inured to the extremes of a life lived close to nature. One frontiersman wrote of seeing Cheyenne, Kiowa, Comanche, and Arapaho children at play on the ice of the upper Arkansas River of Colorado. "The weather is now cold, the river frozen up, the ice a great thickness, and the Indian children . . . are out on the ice by daylight and all as naked as they came into the world," Jacob Fowler noted in 1821. "I doubt that one of our white children, put in such weather in that situation, could live half an hour." [5]

Conflict and Change

For many Indian children harsh weather was less of a danger than other circumstances of their environment. Children were frequent victims of intertribal warfare; they also faced the physical threat brought by the incursion of outsiders on their lands. Early on, bounty-hunting Spaniards received twenty-five dollars for the scalp of each Apache child they brought in, and in later years, children were killed by U.S. cavalry charged with destroying the encampments of "hostile" tribes.[6]

Known to us by her Anglo name, Sarah Winnemucca, Thoc-me-tony, or Shell Flower—was born in the Great Basin of Nevada in the early 1840s at a time when white emigrants were becoming more and more of a presence in the Northern Paiute homelands. By the time she was three, this daughter and granddaughter of Paiute chiefs already had a healthy fear of the newcomers who crossed the plains in ever-greater numbers.

"What a fright we all got one morning to hear some white people were coming," Winnemucca recalled in adulthood. "My aunt said to my mother: 'Let us bury our girls or [they] shall all be killed.' . . . So our mothers buried me and my cousin, planted sage bushes over our faces to keep the sun from burning them, and there we were left." Hardly daring to breathe, the little girls lay in their shallow graves all day, awaiting nightfall and the promised return of their parents. At last the approach of footsteps and the sound of familiar voices signaled an end to their long and terrifying ordeal.[7]

The coming of the whites also endangered Indian children in less direct ways. Natives were especially susceptible to diseases brought by the settlers, diseases against which they had no immunity. Late in 1847 an emigrant train carrying several small children infected with measles arrived in northeastern Oregon. In due time the children of the Cayuse Indians living in the area came down with the disease. While the immigrant children responded well to the medicines given them by Dr. Marcus Whitman, minister and physician at the nearby Waiilatpu Presbyterian mission, the Cayuse children died in large numbers. Nancy Osborn Jacobs, who lived as a child in the mission enclave with her parents, remembered into her old age the keening of a Cayuse father as he cradled the body of his dead child.[8]

Getting the Lay of the Land

For emigrant children like Nancy Osborn Jacobs, life on the frontier was often quite different from what had been expected. The new homesteads on the arid plains of Kansas, Colorado, and the Dakotas or in the valleys of California bore little resemblance to the farmsteads "back home" in Missouri, Minnesota, and Michi-

A Valiant Flight

Above: *Chief Joseph and his family after their attempt to flee to Canada and freedom in 1877, which ended in their incarceration in Indian Territory (Oklahoma).*

Before the close of the nineteenth century the establishment of the reservation system had radically changed the environment of almost every Indian child. The Plains Indians, who had earlier roamed freely over their lands, were successively confined to designated areas by treaty, executive order, or congressional fiat. Even the sedentary tribes—the Mohave, the Papago, and the Modoc—fell under the reservation system.

Under this system, land was set aside as a guaranteed "homeland"—supposedly free of white preemption or trespass—in return for which Indian nations ceded other lands to the United States government. Some tribes received cash payments and/or the promise of annuities, schools, and housing.

Whatever the details of the transaction, a move to the reservation meant an end to a way of life, for under the constant pressures of accommodation and assimilation, native foods, clothes, and customs gradually disappeared.[a]

The inevitability of this loss was immediately apparent to Chief Joseph of the Nez Perce. To avoid confinement on a reservation, he set out in 1877 with a band of some two hundred warriors and about five hundred women, children, and older men on a legendary flight for the Canadian border. Four months later, just shy of his goal and with fewer than three hundred and fifty of his people surviving, Joseph surrendered. The Nez Perce were loaded on a boat and sent down the Missouri River to Fort Abraham Lincoln in Dakota Territory, where a train waited to take them to a reservation in the northeast corner of the Indian Territory, now the state of Oklahoma. As the Northern Pacific engine sounded its whistle, the Indians, who had never seen a train before, set up a mournful keening that sounded to one onlooker like a "death chant."

Soon after their arrival in Oklahoma, the Nez Perce—especially the infants and toddlers—began to show the ill effects of the abrupt environmental change. In a short span of time there were one hundred graves in a cemetery set aside solely for the burial of babies. For years, Chief Joseph lobbied Washington for the return of his people to the Wallowa Valley of eastern Oregon, but the request was never granted.[b]

[a] Richard White, *"It's Your Misfortune and None of My Own": A New History of the American West* (Norman: University of Oklahoma Press, 1991), 91–93; Bowen, *The Indians*, 159.

[b] Geoffrey Ward, ed., *The West: An Illustrated History* (New York: Little, Brown, 1996), 310–23.

gan. Western homesteads were often miles from their nearest neighbors and from the nearest town or settlement.

Though urban centers west of the Mississippi shared some characteristics with eastern towns and cities, the board sidewalks of a mining camp in the Sierras had little in common with the tree-lined sidewalks of an Ohio village. And what of the cultural and language barriers faced by the European immigrant child who took up life on a homestead on the open plains of Nebraska? Or the disorientation felt by the Chinese child transported to the streets of San Francisco or Seattle?

Understandably, there were children who were disappointed in their new environment. Upon arriving at her uncle's ranch in the Santa Clara Valley of California in 1859, eight-year-old Florence Weeks found it a "sorry looking place," noting in her diary, "The first look we had at it

Esther and I cried and asked Uncle to turn around and go straight back to Michigan."[9]

In contrast, thirteen-year-old Martha Gay of Missouri "felt at home" from the moment she, her parents, and eleven siblings arrived in western Oregon in the fall of 1851. The following spring, while her father and brothers completed their new home and fenced, plowed, and planted their forty acres in the Willamette Valley, Martha explored her new surroundings, taking delight in wildflowers and birds she'd never seen before. Friends from Missouri who had preceded her family to Oregon introduced her to the native children of the valley and taught her the jargon that Indian and white children used to communicate with each other. Life out west was all that Martha could have envisioned.[10]

For Mary Sheehan, who was ten in 1863 when she traveled with her family to Montana Territory from Kentucky, a new home

Below: While adults gentle the horses, four children of a Nebraska homesteading family pose for an itinerant photographer. Their well-constructed soddy, the barn, and the windmill show the family's progress toward coaxing a living from the vast, rolling prairie.

Above: After his father and two brothers were killed by Indians, eleven-year-old Merton Eastlick, at the insistence of his wounded mother, fled the family's burning cabin and carried his baby brother, Johnny, fifty miles to safety—and an eventual reunion with his mother, who had survived what would come to be known as the Dakota Conflict of 1862.

in the West offered similar delights. Not long after arriving in Virginia City, the Sheehans were settled in a large log cabin, and Mollie's stepmother was taking in boarders. Though Virginia City was as rough as any other mining camp in the Rockies in 1863, it was also surrounded by natural beauty. With her playmates, two girls her own age also newly arrived in Virginia City, Mollie wandered up the gulches where "the timber lilies bloomed, wild roses and syringa grew in sweet profusion, and flowering currant bushes invited butterflies to alight."

She learned to distinguish fir and pine, juniper and cedar, and she was fascinated by the unfamiliar animals of her new world. "Gophers amused us," she later recalled, "whistling, flipping their tails, and whisking down their holes." She climbed "high up the mountain side," sending "rock-chucks" scurrying away. And on those rare occasions when she and her friends were allowed to go far out on the benchland, they could see antelope in the distance and sometimes a "lone buffalo or the wraith of an Indian smoke signal."[11]

Fears and Friendships

Signs of Indians conjured far different feelings in other children of the frontier. "We children talked about Indians so much it got on my mother's nerves," recalled Mary Gettys Lockard, whose family settled in western Kansas in 1872. Though they had been told that there were no hostile Indians in Kansas, Mary and her siblings had read a book that quoted mountain man Jim Bridger as saying, "Wha're you don't see no Injuns, tha're they are the thickest." That somber quote gave young Mary "the fixed idea that Indians rose up from the ground at times and killed everybody in sight."[12]

Another child of the Kansas frontier, Grace Hays Blackburn, who lived with her parents and siblings in Chase County, soon learned that the Indians who visited their homestead "meant no harm but were only curious." Even so, Grace's mother "never could conquer the sudden fear that gripped her heart" whenever an Indian face "would suddenly and noiselessly appear at the window or door."[13]

Grace's brothers, Charley and Dick Hays, had no such apprehensions. When migrating Kaw Indians camped near their homestead one summer, the Hays boys and friends from nearby farms challenged the Indian youths to endless rounds of jumping and running games. While there is no surviving record as to whom victory most often fell, according to Grace, "the sparkle in their black eyes" testified to the satisfaction gained by the young Kaws.[14]

Olephia King, who grew up in the Monitor Valley of Nevada, organized rodeo games in her corral for herself and the Indian children who lived nearby. And during his family's 1846 move northward from California to Oregon, eight-year-old Benjamin Bonney visited with a group of friendly Indians and eagerly accepted the blackish bread they offered him, thinking it looked somewhat like fruitcake. Even upon learning that the recipe called for crickets and dried acorns rather than raisins and walnuts, Benjamin dutifully downed the bread and pronounced it good.[15]

While children had little to fear from visits from Indians of most tribes, the Sioux and Cheyenne frequently engaged in retaliatory raids, resentful as they were of the invasion of their land by settlers. Having heard rumors of Indian troubles, the Bell and Bogardus families of the Solomon River valley of Mitchell County, Kansas, were gathered in the Bells' small log cabin one hot August morning in 1868 when they were set upon by a band of Cheyenne and Sioux. Three of the adults were killed, and young Esther and Margaret Bell "were strapped on horses with other plunder" and carried off. Miraculously, after a two-day ride south to the Saline River, the raiding party set the girls free. Terrorized, but otherwise unharmed, Esther and Margaret hid in a vacant dugout by the river for a day and a night before being found by other settlers.[16]

The Bell girls experienced—and survived—the worst nightmare of many a westering family. Tales of Indian captivity abounded, especially in the Southwest, where the Apache and Comanche frequently kidnaped settlers—Anglo and Hispanic alike—for later barter with other Indians or traders. The ransom for a child could be high. Comanches at an outpost in Texas demanded "one mare, one rifle, one shirt, one pair of drawers, thirty small packages of powder, some bullets, and one buffalo robe" in exchange for ten-year-old Teodoro Martel. Native children generally brought a lesser price, with the going rate of exchange being a "she mule" or one horse and a "poor bridle . . . garnished with red rags," for an Indian boy and "two good horses and some trifles" for an Indian girl.[17]

Cultural Crossovers

Cultural crossover between Native Americans and Hispanics went beyond bargaining over human "slaves." By the nineteenth century, having already experi-

A Child Who Crossed Cultures

Known today as Sarah Winnemucca, Thoc-me-tony (or Shell Flower) was a child who learned to move with relative ease among the various cultures of her environment. She was born a Northern Paiute in the mid-1840s in present-day Nevada, and her first home was a wickiup—a reed hut with minimal furnishings. In her sixth year she was taken to live with a Hispanic family in the San Joaquin Valley of California, where her home was the adobe hacienda so characteristic of the affluent Californio culture. When she later returned to Nevada, she spent a year as the companion of a stagecoach agent's young daughter, living in the family home—a log structure at a Mormon trading post. Before she reached adulthood, Sarah Winnemucca, née Thoc-me-tony, had become fluent in three languages—Spanish, English, and her native Northern Paiute.[a]

———

[a] Edward James, ed., *Notable American Women* (Cambridge, Mass.: Harvard University Press, 1971), 3:628–29.

enced close contact for almost three centuries, the Spanish and the indigenous cultures shared much in the way of foods, architecture, and agriculture. Both the Zuni and the Hispanic child of the Southwest lived in pueblos, or towns, in homes fashioned from native stone or from adobe—sun-dried mud bricks—though the Zuni child generally lived in a terraced apartment, in a group of buildings piled perhaps five or six stories high, while the Hispanic child most often lived in a single-story home.

The jacal of a poor Hispanic family was a humble abode with whitewashed inner walls and a packed-earth floor that was sometimes covered with a coarse wool rug. Furniture was sparse, sometimes nonexistent, and meals were made of corn products, beans, and the milk and meat from the family's small herd of goats or sheep. In contrast, the massive adobes built by the

Right: In a promotional photograph taken for the Santa Fe Railway at the dawn of the twentieth century, Hispanic children watch an artist painting one of the oldest pueblos in New Mexico.

Below: The children of the José Policarpo Rodriquez family gather with their elders for a picture in front of "The Fort," the family's spacious rancho in Bandera County, Texas. Growing up in the last decades of the nineteenth century, these youngsters lived a life of privileged gentility.

rich rancheros and the Californios attested to the wealth of the families who occupied them. The sixteen children of Francisca and Mariano Vallejo grew up on a 250,000-acre estate in the Sonoma Valley of California. The family owned 50,000 head of cattle, 24,000 head of sheep, and 8,000 horses, and each of the children had his or her own Indian servant whose sole duty was to care for that child.[18]

Early Settlements

While the Vallejo children enjoyed the beauty of their spacious rancho in northern California, some children of Santa Fe, Taos, and other cities of the borderlands West grew up in less-than-lovely environments. Early Los Angeles was described by one observer as "homely almost to ugliness." The clay-colored houses that lined the "crooked and irregular streets" of the pueblo were gloomy and uninviting. The windows lacked glass, and the yards lacked shade-giving trees. The homes had earthen floors and meager furnishings—a few benches, a rawhide-bottomed chair, a rough table, a chest or two. A few pictures of saints might adorn the walls.[19]

Whether located in the Northwest, Southwest, or the mountains of the interior, the typical settlers' town of the early West offered few amenities. Streets were generally unpaved, though in some towns, wooden sidewalks ran in front of the rows of wooden stores lining "Main Street." Many of these business houses had false fronts and wooden awnings. Branching off the main street of the town were dusty side streets, some of which were little more than footpaths. In mining towns like Oatman, Arizona, families lived in houses with

walls and roofs of canvas. Some of these canvas roofs were striped, giving the home, the street, and the town a circus look that delighted Oatman's youngest inhabitants. These dwellings could be surprisingly comfortable. One home in Oatman had burlap-covered walls lined with bookcases. On its linoleum floors sat a Victrola and a piano.[20]

Oatman was an early-twentieth-century version of the older camps of the Sierras and the Rockies, where children, though few in number, were much in evidence, panning along placers abandoned by miners; selling their mothers' baked goods from carts; and hanging around stores, mine entrances, dance halls, and bordellos, all the time taking in the colorful words and ways of the adults who frequented such places.[21]

Mindful of the distractions—and dangers—lurking on the streets of Virginia City, Montana Territory, Mollie Sheehan's

Left: Two boys enjoy a treat from Marcos, the ice cream vendor who plied his trade on the streets of their southwestern town, ca. 1890.

Below: Five small boys proudly line up on the boardwalk in front of a Rocker, Montana, bar to have their pictures taken with the denizens and the proprietor of the establishment. Children of mining camps like Rocker lived in close relationship to the seamier side of the urban environment.

Above: Children join other townspeople outside the rather randomly constructed official residence of the mayor of Ashville, Colorado.

Below: Titled A North Beach Episode *by the artist, Charles Witkowski, this painting of young smokers in a San Francisco alleyway was published by* California Illustrated *magazine in an 1893 article on the ill effects of street life on the city's children.*

stepmother never sent the child out on an errand without cautioning her, "Now run, Mollie, but don't be afraid." The child wondered what there was to fear, for she had known only kindness from the very men who seemed to have the most unsavory reputations among the adults in town. Thus she was shocked and saddened when she rounded a corner one afternoon and saw the limp bodies of five men hanging from the roof beam of a partially constructed cabin. All five were known highwaymen, but two of them, Jack Gallagher and Clubfoot George, she had counted as friends.[22]

Railroad Towns

Railroad towns like Corinne in northern Utah offered the same raw environment as did mining towns like Virginia City. In 1871, the year Eleanor Ferris was born there, Corinne boasted several hundred inhabitants of "varied races, nationalities, and morals"; numerous stores and saloons; one hotel; one little adobe church; and scattered dwellings of wood, adobe, and brick. The daughter of a freighter engaged in establishing rail lines from Utah up through Idaho and into Montana, little Eleanor moved with her family from one "mushroom town" to another. "Our manner of life and that of [these] towns was unique and always temporary," Eleanor Ferris Patten wrote years later in her memoirs. "A town . . . would be established at the particular spot which marked the end of the newly-laid rails, in most cases to remain only until the road was constructed a few miles farther. [Then] the terminus and its dwellers would be moved bodily to the dead end of the railroad, there to remain for a few brief weeks."[23]

Eleanor, her sister, Elizabeth, and her parents were housed at times in large tents and at other times in "crude buildings of rough boards" constructed so that they could be easily taken down, piled onto flatcars, and transferred to the next location. "Thus a whole town could be annihilated and rebuilt almost over night," Patten recalled. "Imagine seeing a long freight train arrive laden with frame houses, boards, furniture, old tents, . . . and all the rubbish of a mushroom town—the guard jumps off—announces that this is Red Rock, Eagle Rock, Camas or whatever name the location suggests and presto!—a new town is built."[24]

Admittedly, Eleanor's father's position meant that she and her family were favored residents of these mushroom towns and were generally lodged in a house "rather more elaborate than the majority." But not, apparently, elaborate enough for cold-weather comfort, since the Ferris girls and their mother spent their winters in San Francisco or the "more mature cities of the East."[25]

The families of Mexican railroad workers in the late-nineteenth-century Southwest endured the heat of summer and the cold of winter housed in boxcars that were shuttled along the rails to wherever the track was being laid. "Their abode," a manager said, "is where these cars are placed." The children who lived in these makeshift homes often worked alongside their parents for the meager wages paid by the Texas and Mexican Railroad in Arizona and by the Southern Pacific Railroad in California.[26]

Racial and Economic Exclusion

The difference in the living environment of the child of affluence and the child of the underclass was especially apparent in the larger cities of the West. One reporter for a turn-of-the-century San Francisco newspaper noted that the two square miles "south of Market street, where live the mechanic, the clerk and the laborer, and where children abound, has one and one-third blocks given over to parks and playgrounds, while the two square miles containing the greatest wealth and the fewest children has twenty-two blocks adorned with parks and open squares."[27]

The children of San Francisco's Chinatown were not even considered in this survey of the city's parks, perhaps because there were so few Chinese children in San Francisco or anywhere else in the nineteenth-century West. Even as late as 1900, 95 percent of Chinese residents in the United States were adult males. The few children to be found in the Chinatowns that sprang up in port cities or in mining and railroad towns across the West—aside from the child prostitutes imported before the Chinese Exclusion Act took effect in 1882—were the children of merchants who either immigrated with or eventually sent for their families. The attitude of most non-Asians toward Chinese children is

evident from a San Francisco journalist's mention of "pig-tailed mites who trot the alley-ways, and jabber in the language of their common fathers."[28]

San Francisco's Chinatown may have been larger than any other such enclave in the West, but it was not unique. Within similar settlements in Seattle and in Butte, Montana, grew a subculture of Chinese stores where whites as well as Chinese came to buy tea, canned fish, and firecrackers—as well as opium and other such esoteric items. Excluded as they were from mainstream frontier society, Chinese children maintained the cultural practices of

Above: A California tent town set up at the end of the line illustrates the living conditions of itinerant rail workers and their families.

Below: These small children making their way unescorted along the streets of San Francisco's Chinatown in the early years of the twentieth century are obviously quite at home moving within the circumscribed world of their own culture within a culture.

Above: The front yard of a sturdy log home in eastern Montana was a playground for Paul and Lucille Burt and an outdoor kitchen for their mother and two friends, who are preparing the midday meal for the sheep-shearing crew. Lady Evelyn Cameron, photographer of early Montana life, captured this scene on a July day in 1905.

their native land in the midst of a foreign environment.[29]

Though they were victims of the same deep prejudice faced by Chinese children, living among their own people on the frontier was not an option for the five offspring of George Washington Bush. A freeman and a well-to-do cattle dealer from Missouri, Bush brought his family west in 1844—only to find they were excluded by law from settling in Oregon country. Undaunted, the Bushes pushed on across the Columbia River to make a home for themselves in the isolated woodlands bordering Puget Sound. Twenty years later, the McDonalds, a free black family with three children from St. Joseph, Missouri, found acceptance among the earliest settlers of Bozeman, Montana Territory. The McDonalds built a log cabin on farmland along Sourdough Creek and were soon established as full-fledged members of the community.[30]

Rural Vistas and Visions

Though cities and towns like San Francisco and Bozeman were an integral part of the frontier scene, for almost every Ameri-

can, the very word "frontier" calls to mind images of a log cabin or sod house on a homestead in the rural West. In truth, only a relatively small number of families who went west were homesteaders in the strict sense of that term. Far more settlers bought their land—though often at prices far below what they would have paid in the East—than earned it under the provisions of the various homesteading acts passed by Congress. Furthermore, there was infinite variety in the structures rural families called home.

For many a family, the wagon in which they had come across the plains became their first frontier home. When twelve-year-old George Jackson, his parents, three sisters, and a brother moved to the Judith Basin of Montana Territory in 1884, they camped that first summer in their covered wagon and two tents. In early fall they were able to move into their new home, a crude cabin equipped with slits in its log walls to accommodate rifle barrels for defense against attack. The family never needed the slits for that purpose, but for George they served as tiny windows onto the starry sky as he lay abed each night.[31]

When thirteen-year-old Martha Gay's family arrived in the Willamette Valley of Oregon in the fall of 1851, they set up housekeeping in the tent city erected by families from their emigration company. Before winter set in, the Gays had moved into the "main part" of the as-yet-unfinished frame house being built by her father and brothers. Over the next few months the large chamber was partitioned into rooms, Oregon maple was fashioned into household furnishings, and "one convenience after another" was added until the family was "quite comfortable."[32]

Born in Norway in 1899, Kaia Lien was five years old when she crossed the Atlantic with her mother, younger brother, and baby sister to join her father in a log cabin on the Yellowstone River in central Montana. The cabin, made of cottonwood trees, had a dirt floor and a dirt roof, from which weeds grew in the summertime. Two apple boxes in one corner of the cabin were the family's cupboard, and other apple boxes served as chairs around the kitchen table made by Kaia's father.[33]

On the plains, where timber was scarce, dugouts and soddies generally served as a

family's first home, with parents and children all living, sleeping, and eating in one small room. Tar-paper shacks provided relatively inexpensive housing for later homesteaders. The fourth child of homesteading parents, Ellen Dute of rural Grand Forks County, North Dakota, was born in a "tar shanty" in Union Township. The home had three rooms: a kitchen, a living room, and a bedroom with three double beds.[34]

Beyond the necessities—a table and benches, a few chairs, a bed or two, somewhere to store clothes and dishes—there was not much furniture in the typical frontier home, and in many cases there was no room for furniture. Magdalena Martin was fourteen in 1909 when her folks left Russia for the prairies of North Dakota. There the nine Martins took up residence with relatives in an abandoned boxcar, living for a year "crowded together like coyotes and their young in a hole."[35]

Crowded quarters were not a problem for a Norwegian family that settled in Basin, Montana. That first summer, the parents and two little girls occupied a log barn that was about two miles up a creek from town

Above: On the Great Plains, where logs and money were scarce and insulation from summer heat and winter chill was essential to comfort—even to survival—sod homes served settlers well. J. W. Speese and his family gather outside their Nebraska soddy in 1888 for Solomon D. Butcher, whose portraits of homesteading families created a rich record of nineteenth-century frontier life.

Clothing, A Product

Achild's environment was often apparent from the clothes he or she wore. Indian babies were encased in sacks fashioned from animal skins. In lieu of diapers, mothers packed the midsections of cradle-boards with soft mosses or the down of cattails. Depending upon the habitat of their tribes, small children were bundled in winter blankets of rabbit, bobcat, or sea otter fur or were dressed in capes of beaver or buckskin. Buckskin leggings warmed their lower extremities, and one-piece moccasins, made from the inside-out skin of the winter buffalo, protected their feet. In warmer seasons Navajo, Apache, and Shoshone children often as not ran naked, though prepubescent girls wore front aprons and at puberty boys donned two-piece buckskin loin cloths.[a]

Settlers' children also often wore clothing made from materials readily available in their environment. For the first few winters after the Applegate family settled in the Willamette Valley of Oregon, the children wore overcoats made from the canvas cover of the wagon that had carried them across the plains. Worn or out-grown clothes were taken apart and stitched into "new" garments. Mothers often took apart their own clothes to refashion them into children's attire. Girls on rural homesteads wore plain and colorless, long-sleeved, high-necked dresses of linsey-woolsey or gingham over their pantalettes and petticoats—and always a sunbonnet. Boys wore heavy boots and long pants and kept their shirts on, no matter how hot the sun.[b]

All the clothes Norwegian immigrants Kaia and Sophie Lien wore were sewn by their mother from material their father brought from town. "My sister and I had dresses made alike, the same kind of material, and we were happy to get those," Kaia Lien Cosgriff remembered. Their mother also knitted their stockings, and with no understanding of allergies, she had little sympathy when Kaia complained about those "nice woolen stockings." "Kaia's the fussiest thing!" her mother would say. "She fusses . . . about everything." "But they make me itch," Kaia would protest. "Well, I just don't

Above: *Hopi children of the Southwest. The girls are dressed in customary woven dresses, shawls, and beads, the little boys in their customary summer na-kedness. The chalkiness apparent on their bodies likely comes from adobe dust.*

Below: *Two little sisters show off their elk-tooth dresses, beads, and buckskin leggings at Powwow Days, Crow Agency, Montana, ca 1905.*

of the Environment

understand that," her mother would declare as she continued to produce the stockings, one pair after the other.[c]

Like almost every other homesteader's child, Urma DeLong Taylor was never allowed to wear her store-bought "dress" shoes except on very special occasions. "Of course, you never wore them around home," Urma remembered. "You only wore them when you went somewhere." As a child raised on a Montana farmstead, Urma had few chances to wear those shoes, but that did not diminish her pride in them.[d]

The clothing of city children varied according to circumstance and culture. Girls' dresses ranged from the simple, serviceable garments of the poor and middle class to the elegant frocks of the wealthy. Belle and Frieda Fligelman, daughters of a Helena, Montana, merchant wore white kid gloves whenever they went downtown. The sisters were ever mindful of the need to keep them clean, and Belle Fligelman Winestine recalled years later, "If we fell down we [had to] remember to fall on our elbows instead of our hands so that we wouldn't spoil our gloves."[e]

[a] *Cycles of Life* (Time-Life), 32; Suttles, *Northwest Coast*, 561–62; *Indians of the Plains* (American Heritage), 41; Craig Doherty and Katherine Doherty, *The Apaches and Navajos* (New York: Franklin Watts, 1989), 51; Warren d'Azevedo, ed., *Great Basin*, vol. 11, *Handbook of North American Indians*, William Sturtevant, ed. (Washington, D.C.: Smithsonian Institution, 1986), 269, 403.

[b] Applegate, *Skookum* 88, 92, 38; Evelyn Toynton, *Growing Up in America, 1830–1860* (Brookfield, Conn.: Millbrook Press, 1995), 32.

[c] Cosgriff interview by Donna Gray, January 8 and 9, 1987.

[d] Urma DeLong Taylor interview by Donna Gray, May 9, 1985 (transcript privately held).

[e] Susan Leaphart, "Frieda and Belle Fligelman: A Frontier-City Girlhood in the 1890s," *Montana The Magazine of Western History* 32 (Summer 1982), 85–92, 86.

Above: *Nine-year-old Dorothea Gans, daughter of a wealthy Helena, Montana, merchant, is dressed to the nines for her studio portrait, ca. 1900. Children's fashions among upper-class families on the urban frontier matched those of their counterparts in East Coast cities.*

Below: *The Hartman twins of Gallatin County, Montana, are dressed for their picture in matching linsey-woolsey dresses and leather button-up shoes.*

Above: A Montana couple show off a new baby in front of their boxcar home near Evaro. Boxcars made suitable dwellings for many of the later homesteaders in the West.

Right: The six children of Annie and Joseph Burkholder, homesteaders from Iowa who settled in Towner County, North Dakota, pose with their parents on the day in 1901 when the family moved out of this tarpaper and sod home and into a spacious, two-story home on the opposite side of their quarter section.

and seasonally vacant while the cows grazed the hillsides. The little girls romped in the pasture while their father found work in the mine and their mother set up housekeeping as best she could in the overly spacious quarters, preparing the family meals on a campfire outside.[36]

Even the more conventional homes were often designed with the kitchen in a lean-to area set apart from the rest of the house, for fire was a very real threat. Once a home caught fire, there was little that could be

done to save it. On a cold winter night in 1893, as the Schumacher family of Stutsman County, North Dakota, huddled around a buffalo-chip fire in the small stove of their one-room cabin, a flying spark ignited straw stacked next to the stove. With the help of their hired hand, Charles and Emilie Schumacher grabbed up the five children in their blankets and dashed toward the barn. Once there, they realized that they had the four little boys, but were missing week-old Clara. On their way back to the burning house, the frantic parents discovered the newborn sound asleep in her feather tick in the snowbank where she had been dropped in the rush from the house.[37]

Natural Disasters

Prairie fires as well as house fires were cause for alarm in a country where high winds could send flames over hundreds of acres in a matter of hours. Winds, combined with drought, brewed dust storms that turned the air brown and covered the world with a fine layer of grit. Flash floods, blizzards, lightning, and tornadoes all posed threats in due season.

Pearl Anderson Granner was an infant in 1887 when a tornado roared out of the south, blowing the roof off her family's home in Grand Forks, Dakota Territory. Her mother gathered up the three children and, shielding them from the flying debris, hustled them to safety down the cellar steps. After the Anderson family moved to a farm outside Emerado, North Dakota, they endured violent thunderstorms. As the winds, rain, and lightning rocked their home, Pearl and her siblings would huddle close as their mother read aloud from the Bible, her voice rising above that of the storm.[38]

Such extremes of weather were a constant threat to families on the frontier. Homesteaders routinely strung a guide rope from house to barn every winter as a precaution against losing one's way while doing chores during a blizzard. Yet for the four young children of John Flannigan, an Irish immigrant and section foreman on the Northern Pacific Railway outside Jamestown, North Dakota, blizzards were the "biggest amusement" available through the long winter months. From within the security of the section house, the Flannigan children watched "the storms play havoc with things about them."[39]

A historic earthquake marked the memories of almost every child living in turn-of-the-century San Francisco. A native of that city, Emma Grapengeter was

six years old on April 18, 1906, when the burgeoning metropolis was nearly destroyed by the quake that struck in the pre-dawn hours. Rushed by her parents from the rubble of their home to the safety of a nearby hillside, Emma watched, mesmerized, as the flames consumed the city below her. "To me, as a child, I thought it was beautiful," she recalled some ninety years later. The "beauty" of that image remained with her throughout the weeks that followed as the Grapengeter family, homeless, lived in the streets and stood in long lines for the food distributed by relief workers.[40]

Above: Two boys stand outside their Oregon home, a log cabin that sports a mud-and-stick chimney and a lean-to kitchen.

Below: An illustration published in Harper's Weekly during the legendary winter of 1886–87 depicts the fate that could befall a frontier family caught in a blizzard.

Above: Children of Butte, Montana, play in their backyard on Center Street in one of a series of photos used in a 1908 report on "insanitary" living conditions in the mining town. The investigator's penciled "X" was intended to highlight "a pile of soiled clothes."

Illness and Accidents

Epidemics of whooping cough, scarlet fever, measles, and diphtheria swept through gold rush communities and carried off whole families. All three children of one Caribou, Colorado, couple died within four days of one another in 1879, and a Colorado mother lost two children in as many months to scarlet fever and meningitis. Minnie Brown, of Roseburg, Oregon, survived scarlet fever as a child of seven only to die of typhoid fever at fourteen.[41]

Accidents as well as disease threatened the lives of children. In mining camps little ones tumbled into shafts, fell into swift-running streams, and strayed into the paths of horses and ore wagons. "This is an awful place for children," one mother wrote after settling in Rich Bar, California.[42]

Even in the seemingly healthful environment of rural homesteads, children were not immune from accidents, and mothers living in relative isolation were often obliged to treat their children without the benefit of professional medical care. When Olephia King of Monitor Valley, Nevada, broke her arm in a game of "rodeo" in the home corral, her mother packed the limb in mud for an hour, then splinted it with wooden slats taken from an apple box found in the barn.[43]

Animal Adversaries

Frontier children sometimes faced unexpected encounters with wild animals. When Charline Sackett, a Wyoming ranch child, dropped to her knees one morning to look under her bed for her missing doll, she found herself staring into the eyes of a coiled snake inches away from her face. Hypnotized by the snake's gaze—or paralyzed by her own fear—Charline remained motionless for what seemed an eternity. The impasse was finally broken when her mother entered the room, saw the little girl crouched on the floor, and grabbed her up just as the snake struck. Charline's father cornered and killed the reptile—"a seven-foot rattler, fully as large around as an average man's arm."[44]

Many a settler's child wandered by accident into a den of rattlers. When Martha and Mamie Gay found themselves at the mouth of such a den near their homestead in the Willamette Valley in Oregon, they themselves killed five of the snakes before

running home to enlist the aid of their older brothers in dispatching as many more snakes as they could. The Lien children would not likely have engaged in such a hunt, considering their mother's live-and-let-live attitude toward the rattlers living on their homestead along Montana's Yellowstone River. "[The snakes] were just thick," Kaia Lien Cosgriff recalled. "[But] my mother didn't kill them. She'd say, 'Now, kids, you'd better let the rattlesnakes have this territory and move over there. . . .' To this day," Cosgriff marveled in later life, "I don't know how we escaped being bit by rattlesnakes."[45]

Cougars, or mountain lions, were also a part of the environment. In rural Lane County, Oregon, two children, ages ten and twelve, drove a wagon into town to pick up some barrels of cement for their father. At dusk, as they were driving toward home down the timbered road, a cougar jumped on the wagon, startling horses, driver, and passenger and knocking the barrels onto the ground. Setting their team to a gallop, the children arrived home safely but without the cement, a loss their father readily excused.[46]

Above: Children play outside their dugout home near McCook, Nebraska, in the 1890s. Note the root cellar on the far left, the scatter of sticks the children have gathered for fuel, the rain barrel and washtub on the right, and the blur of wind-whipped linens on the clothesline atop the mound. What a dugout home lacked in aesthetics was more than made up for by its being virtually windproof—an essential trait for homes on the open plains, especially during winter.

Below: The pollution pumped over the city by the copper-smelting plants is easily visible in this 1889 stereopticon view of Butte, Montana.

Above: *The influx of settlers led to clashes between humans and animals. These young marksmen, Raymond and Gilbert Lord, have brought down a pair of cougars that were stalking the livestock on their family's western Montana ranch.*

Opposite, above: *A group of Russian immigrants, having just arrived by train in Bismarck, North Dakota, in 1900, are waiting for transportation to their new homes on the prairie.*

Opposite, below: *The Ole I. Gjevre family, Norwegian immigrants, pose outside their board-and-sod house in Osnabrock Township, North Dakota, 1898.*

Even domesticated animals could frighten children. Five-year-old George Knox, the proud owner of a tasseled red cap his English grandmother had brought him, could not go out into the farmyard without having the hat snatched from his head by a large gander. One day, having endured enough from the "mean son-of-a-gun," George grabbed up a board and took off after the gander, determined to reclaim his hat. "We met somewhere out there in the yard," he later recalled. By his own report, George "wasn't doing so good" in the fray until a friend who was a little older and a little stronger came to his rescue.[47]

Strangers in a Strange Land

Nine-year-old Christine Hinderlie was a carefree, adventuresome little girl when she left Norway with her parents in 1884 in search of a better life in the New World. The joy she anticipated finding in that world never materialized. Ellis Island was a "fearful experience" in which she and her family—none of whom understood En-glish—were driven "like cattle" through the great hall by immigration officials. Her arrival at their isolated farm in eastern South Dakota only increased Christine's sense of dislocation, for "Everything was new and queer to us who were used to living in a town."[48]

Young Christine found the reptiles and rodents of this new world so "deathly scary" that she felt as if "all the fun was taken out of life." Sent on an errand across the fields to the family's nearest neighbor, Christine heard a rustling in the thick grass behind her and realized something was following her. Turning around, she gave one swift kick to the stalker and ran on, never looking back. On her return trip through the field, she discovered the lifeless body of her own kitten and realized what she had done. At that moment, everything about her new world seemed terribly wrong.[49]

Not all immigrant children experienced the depression and isolation known by Christine Hinderlie. Though they too had no knowledge of the language, customs, or foods of their adopted country, the Liens adapted as best they could to life in central Montana. Once, when neighbors brought a basket of bright red tomatoes to the homestead, Kaia Lien's mother dutifully thanked them. But as soon as the neighbors departed, she warned the children that they could not taste the strange fruit until she herself had sampled it. As the three youngsters gazed up at her, she took a bite out of a plump tomato and promptly spat out the sour-tasting morsel. "It's poison!" she declared, and hurried to throw the tomatoes away. It would be years before Kaia herself knew the taste of a tomato.[50]

Overly cautious as Kaia Lien Cosgriff's mother may have been, hers was a caution shared by many other parents who realized that life in a frontier environment required vigilance, resilience, perseverance, and ingenuity, traits young Kaia and countless other frontier children learned by precept and example within the family circle.

The Family Circle

Frontier Children within the Home

Although the treatment a frontier child received within the family circle was subject to many variables—including parental temperament—by and large, parents in all the cultures of the American West valued children. In almost every Native American tribe a child was considered a gift from the Great Mystery, and most settlers tended to look upon an infant as a blessing from God.[1]

Among homesteaders, for whom strong and healthy children meant extra hands to help in the establishment of a self-sustaining farm, families of six to twelve children were not uncommon. For some Californios, having large families was considered a mark of status—"the larger the family circle the more important the family." And generally speaking, the larger the brood, the greater the hedge against the frontier's high infant and child mortality rates.[2]

For whatever reasons, Native Americans tended to have fewer children, and when Ohiyesa, a young Sioux, heard that a German immigrant family close by his clan's encampment numbered nine children, he could not help wondering why "the Big Knives increase so much more in number than the Dakotas."[3]

Cradleboard Culture

While the families of settlers generally had more children, Indian families invariably numbered more adults, for a native child was born into an extended family that embraced not only his or her parents and blood relatives but indeed all members of the band or clan. A Sioux boy would address all of his father's brothers and cousins as "father," and all the adults in a clan saw to the welfare of the children. In some tribes a paternal relative even bore the responsibility for naming an infant at birth.[4]

Indian babies spent most of the daytime hours of their first year in a cradleboard, a wooden frame with a pouch made of soft animal skin. A versatile device, the cradleboard could be carried on the mother's back, hooked over a pommel, strapped to a travois, hung up inside a tipi, or leaned against a tree. At night some infants were placed in deerskin cradles hung on poles high above the floor of the tipi, while others lay on the ground, snuggled in soft buckskin bags. Despite the seeming confinement of long days spent strapped to the board, the Indian infant developed sitting, crawling, and walking skills in the usual sequence and in the same time frame as did the unconfined Anglo or Hispanic child.[5]

Cradleboard designs and decorations varied from tribe to tribe. In some groups, cradleboards were painted different col-

Opposite: An early-twentieth-century family of the Glendale, Oregon, area.

Below: With the help of her mother, who stands behind her, and a very patient pony, this Cayuse toddler is introduced to the art of horsemanship.

What's in a Name?

Afraid Eagle

Slow Bear

An Indian boy's birth name was usually given with the implicit understanding that it would be changed at appropriate times in the child's life—with his first steps, for instance, or on the occasion of his first hunt. Girls more often kept the name given at birth, though there were girls who earned new names during their growing-up years. Strange Child—so called at birth by her Modoc kin because of her fine, reddish-brown hair—was canoeing on the Klamath River with friends one day when their craft was swept into dangerous rapids. Calming her playmates, Strange Child guided the canoe past boulders and into quiet waters. It was through this childhood act of courage that she became Winema, "Stout-Hearted Woman."[a]

Among the Cheyenne, a boy was named for an animal or a physical attribute: Tall Bull, for example, or Spotted Wolf, while a girl's name almost always had "Woman" in it: Owl Woman or Little Creek Woman. Among the Pueblo people, girls were named for plants and flowers, boys for animals or athletic skills. Names such as these, based as they were on physical objects, were easily rendered by pictograph.[b]

A young child often acquired a nickname that persisted for the first five or six years of life—sometimes longer—or until some special event occasioned another naming ceremony. For example, as a young lad, Jumping Badger, son of a Hunkpapa chief, was nicknamed Hunkesni, or "Slow," because of his deliberate manner, a sobriquet he retained into his teen years—when he became Sitting Bull, the name by which he is known to us today.[c]

---

[a] Bowen, *Indians*, 85, 89; d'Azevedo, *Great Basin*, 352; Gridley, *American Indian Women*, 61–62.

[b] Bowen, 85–87, 89; Alfonso Ortiz, ed., *Southwest*, vol. 9, *Handbook of North American Indians*, ed. William Sturtevant (Washington, D.C.: Smithsonian Institution, 1979), 273.

[c] Utley, *Lance and Shield*, 5–6.

Right: *Like the children of other Native American tribes, these Shoshone youngsters from the Wind River basin in Wyoming were nurtured and guided by an extended family, including tribal leaders. Washakie, the chief of this clan, is seen on the far left.*

ors—white for boys, yellow for girls—or decorated with different objects—feathers for boys, beads for girls—to accent an infant's gender. The covering of the boy's board had a penis hole, allowing the child to urinate outside the pouch.[6]

In many tribes twins were considered, at best, an imbalance of nature and, at worst, a sign of impending bad luck. Among the Western Shoshone and the Utes, a twin—sometimes both twins—was neglected at birth and left to die.[7] But with the singular exception of twins, Native American infants were generally coddled, allowed to nurse at will, and pampered by all their kin. They were not, however, allowed to cry, for an infant's cries could pose danger to the whole tribe by alerting enemies to the camp's location. A baby who continued to cry after its needs had been met was hung in its cradleboard from a bush or tree outside the camp and left there to cry itself out. When the howling stopped, the baby was brought back into camp. After a few such experiences, the infant learned that

crying was useless and thus took its first step toward self-control, a virtue highly valued in Indian society.[8]

By the age of two or three, youngsters were on horseback, either riding with their mothers or riding alone tied in a saddle on a gentle horse led by an adult. By five or six a boy might have his own pony and be sent out to herd the horses; girls of the same age helped their mothers dig roots and carry water and wood.[9]

The ceremonies marking a child's passage through life varied from tribe to tribe. Among the Apaches the child's first haircut, given when it had outgrown its cradleboard, was generally performed by the band's medicine man or woman. The hair was cut—sometimes burned—very short, though a few long strands were left. This initial trim might well be the only one the child would ever receive, for haircuts after childhood were thought to bring bad luck. At age two an Apache child was given moccasins in a ceremony that entailed exchanges of gifts and a day-long

Above: These twins—captured in a split-second change of mood—were born to Cayuse parents in Oregon. The Cayuse, unlike some tribes, did not fear multiple births and showed more tolerance for crying babies than did the Plains Indians, for whom a crying child was a danger and a distraction. Note the beads decorating the cradleboards and the penis hole in the little boy's rigging.

Above: Dressed in a fine bonnet and surrounded by warm furs, little Ella Bernice Allderdice of Chouteau County, Montana, is taken for an airing in her home-crafted baby carriage.

Below: Little Hannah Elizabeth Ottinger, born in 1869, was wheeled about the streets of Salt Lake City in this elegant pram. Note the dainty parasol, used to shade her face when the pram faced the sun.

celebration. At the age of seven both the boys and the girls of the Tsimshian tribe of the Pacific Northwest went through their first initiation rites, at which time the ears of the little girls were pierced.[10]

Varied Expectations and Experiences

The achievements of settlers' children were also celebrated, though there were no elaborate ceremonies to mark baby's first steps, first word, or first haircut. Rather, news of a child's progress was noted by proud parents and remarked upon in letters sent to friends and families back east or in the mother country. Lillie Fergus Maury, who had followed her husband to a homestead in Iowa, sent her mother in Montana Territory detailed accounts of little Marion's progress: "We always sing when we rock him to sleep. Lately he has tried to sing; keeps making a noise when we sing. He can almost sit alone, turns over himself and sucks his fist."[11]

Children were generally kept at a discrete distance during the arrival of a new sibling. However, an Oregon woman who went into labor while her husband was temporarily away from the homestead found herself in a difficult dilemma. With no one available to fetch the midwife or to watch after her two little girls while she went through labor, she had the girls, aged five and three, bring to her bedside a basket of apples that stood in a corner in the kitchen. Then, from the vantage point of her bed, she rolled one apple after another across the bedroom, through the kitchen, and out into the yard, sending the little girls into peals of laughter as they chased after and retrieved the bright red fruit while their mother delivered their baby sister.[12]

Settlers' children knew harsh discipline as well as gentle care. The Schumacher boys of Stutsman County, North Dakota, were brought up under their father's buggy whip. A stern man with a harsh temper, Charles Schumacher saw almost any offense, no matter how slight, as an occasion for punishment. For each infraction, a child was made to fetch the whip and stand stoically to receive his lashes. If a boy should attempt to escape the whip, it only meant additional punishment.[13]

One of the strongest impressions some frontier children retained of their childhood was of the harshness of home life. "At table we weren't supposed to talk," the children of North Dakota homesteaders Rosina and Johann Schmidt remembered. "It was always 'Ess, ess!' [Talk during meals] was a waste of time." The father of this brood had "an iron hand," and his oldest son endured his last beating as a seventeen-year-old. But beatings did not always come at the hands of a father. One woman remembered her mother as being "quick with her punishment if you didn't do . . . right." In attempting to rationalize the strict discipline she had known as a child, this woman acknowledged that her mother had "had a big load to carry and got pretty tired sometimes." There was, as a result, only the most tenuous bond between mother and daughter. "In a big family if you had a problem you went to your older sister or brother," this woman remembered. "You didn't go to mother."[14]

But sometimes a mother was the only protection a child had, especially when a drunken father became abusive. When Jessie Dillon was five years old, her mother finally sought a divorce from the alcoholic physician who had made their lives miserable. "When my husband . . . was drunk," Elizabeth Paschal Dillon testified, "which was most of the time, he would worry Jessie till she cried and then he would beat her for crying."[15]

Marvin Powe's father likely intended no abuse toward his son, even while forcing responsibility on him far beyond his age. Marvin, who grew up on a New Mexico ranch, was only nine when he was sent out to look for some runaway horses. Knowing better than to come home empty-handed, the boy tracked the horses far beyond the borders of their ranch, "living off the land

and camping for a while with some cowboys." Though a full week passed before Marvin located the horses and returned home, trailing the herd, his father expressed only mild concern over the length of his absence, having fully expected the boy to persevere until he had fulfilled his responsibility.[16]

The word "responsibility" had no such connotations for the privileged Californio child. With festivity a way of life, even washday expeditions that began before sunrise and ended near dusk were occasions for frolic. Joyful jumbles of children trooped alongside the carretas and packhorses that carried baskets piled high with laundry to the nearby warm springs. There

Above: The four offspring of Isaac and Anna Miller were born in a mining camp in the Sierra Nevadas, but by the time this studio portrait was made in 1873 they were living on a farm in central California. Since their German-born mother spoke no English and their American-born father spoke no German, the Miller children bridged two cultures and assumed many responsibilities at an early age.

Above: *Juana Elias of Arizona is shown in her first communion picture in 1901. Religious ritual was a major component in the lives of Hispanic children.*

prepare for the post-christening feast. In one case, the tiny honoree nearly missed its own party. The godparents had set out for the church one cold New Mexico morning with the baby riding behind them in an improvised bed on the floor of the wagon. As the wagon pitched and jolted its way to the church, the baby was tossed out onto the frozen ground. Only belatedly discovering the loss, the godparents turned the team around and retraced their route, finding the squalling infant a few miles back.[18]

The festivities surrounding a child's baptism were repeated with the celebration of his or her first communion some seven years later. Again, the godparents played a major role in the rite, for they shared with the parents the responsibility for supervising the spiritual and moral welfare of the child.[19]

Though generally lacking the festive character of Hispanic celebrations, the Sunday church services enjoyed by settlers' families provided a welcome break from the week's labors. For most settlers, the establishment of a community church was a high priority, and with so few other opportunities for interaction with neighbors, a frontier family's social life often centered around weekly religious activities.

The faith that drew Mormon families west helped sustain them during their struggle to turn arid acres into bounteous fields. The children of the Latter-day Saints grew up in a theocracy, a world in which there were no secular activities. Even the most isolated hamlet had a hall in which worshipers could gather, and the completion of the temple in Salt Lake City was a goal shared by all believers. From an early age, Mormon children attended religious education classes that helped prepare them for the societal roles they would one day assume. And since many of these children grew up in a family complex that included the plural wives of their fathers, the tenets of their religion had a direct effect on the structure and dynamics of the family circle.

the children played and picnicked until time to return to the ranch house. Hispanic children of the Southwest—rich and poor alike—enjoyed the many fiestas of the region. These celebrations, with singing, dancing, and feasting, were generally coupled with elaborate religious processions in celebration of some saint's day.[17]

Frontier Religion

The lives of most frontier children were affected, to some degree, by the religious observances advocated by their parents. Hispanic families considered a child's baptism cause for great celebration. On the day of the christening, the baby, decked out in all of its new finery, was carried by its godparents to the parish priest, while the rest of the household stayed behind to

Certificate of Baptism.

This Certifies, That *Blanche Viola*
child of *Ezra* and *Elizabeth Anderson*
born *July 14th* *1881*, has this day been

BAPTISED

into the name of the Father, the Son and the Holy Ghost.
She is thus acknowledged as a child of the Church, a child
of the Covenant, to be faithfully, carefully, prayerfully "brought
up in the nurture and admonition of the Lord."

"And if ye be Christ's then are ye Abraham's seed and
heirs according to the Promise."

Ezra Anderson
Elizabeth Anderson } Parents.

F. Doran
Pastor.

Methodist
Presbyterian Church Grand Forks D.T., June 13 1886

Left and above: *Methodist Baptismal Certificate and photo of Blanche Viola Anderson of Grand Forks, Dakota Territory, June 1886.*

Though the isolation of frontier life was tempered for Mormon children by the social structure of the church, for most other homesteading children that isolation was keenly felt. Born in 1863 to parents who had settled near Walla Walla, Washington Territory, Cora Clark "never had any church services, Sunday school, or anything of the kind." And Martha Gay, newly settled in the Willamette Valley of Oregon in 1851, was shocked to see neighboring children so distanced from society, and "so wild," that they not only did not go to Sunday school but even told her that they did not care to go.[20]

Fearing just such "wildness" on the frontier, churches in the States sent hundreds of missionaries west to evangelize settlers and Native Americans alike. Indian children who had grown up believing in deities who resided everywhere—in sky, sun, moon, earth, and rock, in wind and lightning, in deer and buffalo—deities with whom one could, indeed must, interact on

Above: *The influence of plural marriages in past generations is subtly apparent in this turn-of-the-century Romney family gathering in Salt Lake City. The little boy whose birthday is being celebrated is surrounded by only a few of his 125 first cousins.*

Right: *The Kiowa children gathered around the Reverend J. J. Methvin sometime in 1894 were likely more intrigued with the bicycle on which the Methodist missionary traveled between his mission posts than with the testimony by which he sought to persuade them to give up their traditional spiritual beliefs in favor of Christianity.*

a daily basis, were admonished by priests and ministers to renounce these "pagan gods" and learn to keep the Sabbath.[21]

As members of the Jewish community of Helena, Montana, the Fligelman girls "kept the Sabbath" on Saturday rather than on Sunday. "[T]here were many things that we were not allowed to do [on that day]," Belle Fligelman Winestine remembered years later, "including sewing on our doll clothes." Despite this proscription, one Saturday afternoon while their stepmother was napping, Frieda and Belle got out their doll clothes and were sewing "like anything" when they heard their stepmother's approach. Hastily hiding their work, the two were empty-handed by the time she entered the room. "Children, you've been sewing," Getty Fligelman said at once. Not realizing that they had left scraps of cloth on the floor, the little girls denied the charge. "Yes, you have," their stepmother insisted. "God has written it on your forehead." Startled by this knowledge and yet unable to see the telltale marks themselves, Frieda and Belle were ever after strict observers of the Sabbath.[22]

"Sunday was [the] worst day" of the week for the Lien children, Norwegian immigrants who grew up on the plains of central Montana. "Mother would clean us up," Kaia Lien Cosgriff recalled. "We'd sit on these boxes [and] she'd read the Bible to us, almost all day. . . .Oh, we hated Sundays because you couldn't do anything but sit there and listen." Even so, there were some long-term advantages to the dreaded practice. "The stories that she read to us, and the songs that she sang to us," Cosgriff admitted years later, "they're still with me."[23]

For Katherine Elspeth Oliver, a child of Kansas pioneers, Sunday nights were "best of all." Then the family gathered around the melodeon that had accompanied them west from New York. "Mother used to play as we sat in the twilight and far into the dark, the lamps unlighted." For the whole family, Sunday was "a day full of delightfully different things," and Oliver especially cherished memories of "the long drive to 'town' [for] church and Sunday school and [then the] picnic lunch eaten in the wagon on the way home."[24]

Family Diversions

Picnics were always a favorite frontier activity, especially when shared with other families. Hungry children filled their plates from a cloth laden with baskets of chicken, platters of ham, bowls of vegetables, and an array of breads, relishes, cakes, and pies. After a leisurely lunch, older children took part in ball games, footraces, or singing, while the younger ones played games of jump rope, tag, or hide-and-seek.[25]

Sometimes just going to town was cause

Above: *Children fill the scene at this gathering of Nebraska homesteaders outside their sod church. Church membership filled a social as well as a religious need for frontier families, though Sunday services were usually more eagerly anticipated by adults than by children.*

Above: *Several generations of the Neely family of Florence, Oregon, enjoy a Sunday evening of music and storytelling, with the little boys showing great patience as they wait expectantly for the treat their grandmother is preparing.*

enough for celebration—especially for children who made that journey only once a year. "Sam and I would sit in the back [of the wagon]," Kaia Cosgriff remembered, "you know, just a little cubbyhole in the back with our feet hanging out. Oh, we were in seventh heaven!"[26]

Urma DeLong Taylor, another child of frontier Montana, recalled waiting impatiently for her mother to hitch the team to the wagon for a trip into town, an outing that usually meant "a few sticks of candy, a few little odds and ends." But on one very significant day, Urma came home with a pair of shoes, "bought out of the catalog," that were waiting for her at the post office. "Oh, those leather shoes!" she remembered years later. "You know what new leather smells like. That was the best perfume I'd ever smelled as a child. As we went along, every few minutes I'd take them out— ohhh—put them on and look them over,

then put them back in the box . . . [all] the way home."[27]

Before they built a community house, the families of Lane County, Oregon, would gather almost weekly in a neighbor's living room, roll up the rug, and dance til daylight to the music of banjo and fiddle. Little Gertrude Knox loved such affairs. In the early part of the evening, there was lots to see and overhear, but as the night wore on, she and the other children would "crawl onto a bed someplace amongst all the coats and go to sleep." Then, in the predawn hours, the sleepy-headed youngsters would be picked up and bundled into wagons, so parents would be home in time to do the morning chores.[28]

Gertrude Knox also recalled "going to a dance in the middle of winter" in the big, unfinished hall of the newly constructed community house. With no beds on which to lie, the children stretched out

Left: *In 1894 a bevy of children, dressed in their party best, gathered at the Lucas home in Santa Maria, California, to surprise Lee Lucas, son of the town physician, on the occasion of his tenth birthday. Beside the traditional cake and ice cream, the partygoers enjoyed generous platters of berries and fruits from nearby farms and orchards.*

Below: *In frontier towns devoid of family entertainment beyond that afforded by church and school gatherings, excitement reached fever pitch with the arrival of the circus. Impatient for the show to begin, these children of early Denver—and an adult or two—peer under the Big Top, hoping to hurry the roustabouts.*

under the benches that lined the walls, and from that vantage point they observed their elders at play, although "all [they] could see was ankles."[29]

Little Besse Gupton loved to go to dances in the homes of neighbors who lived near her family's ranch outside Gillette, Wyoming. Having surreptitiously followed some older girls upstairs one evening, she waited until they had gone back down, then proceeded to drape herself in the jewelry they had left behind.

Her grand entrance—made with one string of beads wound around her waist, another around her neck, and several around her arms—was prelude to an abrupt exit as her father ushered her back upstairs to return the "fancies."[30]

The coming of the circus to town was sure to generate much excitement in frontier children. Even as a five-year-old, Mary Rowe of Victor, Montana, was up and on her way to town with her family before dawn to watch the circus train unload. The

Above: In Tulare County, California, loggers and their partners pause for the photographer during a two-set quadrille performed on an unusual dance floor. The younger members of the community wait to be free of the photographer's commands so they can resume their own forms of entertainment.

whole day was full of excitement—from the acts under the big top to the fifteen-cent bags of hard candies bought from the vendor. County and state fairs also drew families in from the countryside. Martha Gay's family "never failed to attend the Oregon State Fair." Those fairs "were well worth going sixty miles to see," she said, "even if we did have to go in a wagon and camp out and do our own cooking." The sights and sounds and smells and tastes of the fair stayed with her for a lifetime, as did memories of "the fine cattle, horses, sheep, goats, pigs, chickens and turkeys . . . the grains of all kinds, the fruits and garden vegetables, the butter and Oregon cheese."[31]

Holidays

The Fourth of July was a major celebration for western communities, complete with political speeches, horse races, foot-races, ball games, pie-eating contests, shooting contests, dancing, and parades. The celebration in Lewistown, Montana,

brought in everyone from the surrounding country. For this special trip to town, rigs were spruced up with fresh paint, and high-stepping "driving" horses were brought out. In the mining community of Oatman, Arizona, Fourth of July celebrations that lasted up to three days included something for everyone. Of greatest interest to most residents was the rock-drilling contest in which teams from all across the territory competed for prize money.[32]

For Harriet Cowle Walter, born in Kansas in 1873, the Fourth was the best day of the year. Her family always got up early in order to hear the salute that was "fired in every town at sun up," and morning chores were quickly dispatched. Then they all piled into the wagon for the ride into town, wih "little flags" fluttering from the bridles of the horses. "What a day it was," Walter recalled. "There was a float filled with as many little girls as we had states, little girls dressed in white with sashes and caps of red, white, and blue."[33]

In a similar parade down Virginia City's

Above: *A state fair could entice home-steading families to travel great distances to exhibit their produce, livestock, canned goods, and handiwork; to enjoy the midway; or, in the case of the 1913 Montana State Fair in Helena, to enter their most precious products in the baby contest.*

Left: *The Loughrey, Erskine, and Bean families of Gallatin Valley, Montana, gather for a Fourth of July picnic in 1893. The Fourth was always an occasion for celebration—sometimes in town with speeches, bands, and games, sometimes at home or on a creek bank with family and friends.*

Above: Christmas 1910 brought a rocking horse and a new doll and doll furniture to three-year-old Lee and six-year-old Helen Nash of Helena, Montana.

main street in Montana Territory on the Fourth of July, 1865, Mollie Sheehan was one of thirty-five little girls, all clad in white, who rode on a mule-drawn wagon bedecked with evergreens and bunting and presided over by an older girl dressed as Miss Liberty. [34]

No other frontier holiday compared with Christmas in the mind of a child—or in the memory of an adult. "They had the tree there and all the little candles on it, just little candles," Herb Mickelson recalled of a turn-of-the-century Christmas during his childhood in Butte, Montana. "The ornaments for the tree were mostly homemade: strings of popcorn, strings of cranberries, walnuts wrapped in tinfoil. There'd be a few little [store-bought] ornaments. One present and a little bag of candy. We were satisfied. It was still Christmas and we had a big feast."[35]

On December 26, 1860, twelve-year-old Bella Williams of Homer, Iowa, wrote to tell her brother of the holiday celebration the family had enjoyed at a neighbor's: "We had an excellent dinner at three o'clock, of which a seventeen pound turkey was the most conspicuous, a 'taffy . . . pulling' in the evening, and then we played 'Bachelor' and 'Quaker' till ten o'clock, when we [ate again], and then waded home through the snow, to a cold house and tumbled into equal[l]y cold beds, slept till five, and then tumbled out again to go through the daily ro[u]tine."[36]

Among Hispanic families of the Southwest, the Christmas season was so eagerly anticipated that the month in which the celebration fell was referred to not as December but as *el mes de Noche Buena,* or the month of Christmas Eve. Throughout the month, youngsters were kept on good behavior through fear of El Abuelo (the Grandfather). During the week before Christmas, El Abuelo, sporting grotesque makeup and a mask, would appear in various villages and pueblos. Knocking on doors, cracking his whip, and addressing the parents of cowering, speechless children, he would roar, "Han sido buenos muchachos estos?" (Have these children been good?)[37]

Predictably, the parents would assure El Abuelo that their *ninos* had been very good and that he should not carry any of them off. Placated, El Abuelo would accept a glass of wine or some other refreshment, then move on to the next house. In a region where Spanish and Indian legends blended into one, the highlights of Christmas were El Abuelo's visits, the luminarias—cheerful little wood bonfires placed in front of every home to light the way for the Christ Child—and a plethora of good foods.[38]

While their neighbors celebrated Christmas, Jewish children across the West enjoyed the family rituals associated with Hanukkah, the Feast of Lights. Then, in the fall, they observed Rosh Hashanah, the Jewish New Year. Mary Goldsmith Prag, who was six years old in 1852 when she left her native Poland for California, never forgot her first Rosh Hashanah service in San Francisco when she and her sister sat in the gallery of Sherith Israel temple.[39]

The Chinese New Year, observed according to the Chinese lunar calendar in late

Above: A frontier family gathers for the Thanksgiving meal in Powell, Wyoming, in 1910.

Left: Chinese children dressed in their New Year's best prepare to carry an old-world custom into the streets of San Francisco.

Opposite, below: In 1898 the people of Kalispell, Montana, were treated to a Fourth of July pageant staged by the town's children. Celebrations of this sort were common across the frontier.

Above: Three-year-old Eddie Thornton was pulling a watermelon in his wagon down the main street of Grants Pass, Oregon, one morning in 1890 when D. F. Everitt, a photographer just setting up his studio in town, called him in to sit for this portrait. Upon hearing of Eddie's death a few days later, Everitt gave the picture to the boy's mother, who had no other picture of her son and did not know that this one had been taken.

A Death in the Family

The frontier family frequently faced the loss of a child or a parent to illness or accident. In 1898, Norwegian immigrants Martha and Ole Lima of Cooperstown, North Dakota, lost their two-year-old daughter, Gunhild, to whooping cough. Coping with the death of "this beautiful and lovable child" had been "hard beyond measure" for them all, Ole wrote home to Norway. Three-year-old David would wake at night "in bitter weeping." He and Gunhild had been close playmates, and just days before her death, the little girl had "sat in the cradle with a little bottle" and sung to David. "Afterward," the distraught father wrote, "she asked, 'Dave, did you like that?'"[41]

When scarlet fever struck the Dute family of rural Grand Forks County, North Dakota, little Ellen was too young to understand the seriousness of the situation. "I remember taking sick, crawling into bed, turning my face to the wall, and wanting to be left alone," she later recalled. But that wish was denied, for her two sisters and baby brother, also stricken, soon shared her sickbed. When the baby died and the undertaker came to the house, little Ellen could not understand why her parents would permit the stranger with "a very ugly face . . . [to] carry the baby away."[42]

The death of a young cousin who was living with the Gay family in Greene County, Missouri, in 1849 puzzled Martha Gay and her siblings, who "had never seen a dead person before. . . . We did not know why little Sarah was so cold and still," Martha recalled. "But when they put her in a little casket which father made and buried her away off in . . . the orchard under a peach tree we realized she . . . would be with us no more."[43]

Two-year-old Mathilda Martin, youngest child of German-Russian immigrants to North Dakota in the early years of the twentieth century, did not survive her first year in the new country. With the family crowded into a boxcar and the parents

January or February, prompted festivities that lived on in the memory of Collin Dong, son of a restaurateur on the Monterey peninsula in California. Dong remembered how his mother would dress him and his siblings in "colorful costumes," and his father, "dressed in his best Chinese silken gown," would accompany them as they went from door to door, paying their respects to other families of the Chinese community. Those on whom the children called would hand them "little red packages containing 25-cent pieces, called *li shee*." "After a day's collection of these red packages," Dong realled, "our pockets were usually quite full." Adults tended to be generous, since those who gave *li shee* were assured of good luck in the coming year.[40]

scrambling for survival, the care of the sickly child fell mainly to her oldest sister, fourteen-year-old Magdalena. Concerned neighbors offered what "medicines" they had—herbs, teas, goose-lard liniments. Catholic neighbors blessed the child with the sign of the cross, and Protestant neighbors offered comforting words from the Scriptures. But the toddler languished. Then one evening, as Lena was lifting Mathilda into bed the frail little body went limp. The baby had died in her arms.[44]

The healing arts practiced in an Indian encampment were somewhat similar to those used by settlers on the rural frontier. When an Apache or Navajo child fell sick, the medicine man or woman offered an appropriate chant and applied specific herbs.[45] When all else failed, Indian parents sometimes turned to the "medicine" of other cultures. On the Northern Cheyenne reservation in Montana Territory, Ursuline nuns who staffed the mission school were urged by an Indian father to ask the Great Spirit to cure his desperately ill child. Taking along "holy water and a crucifix," the nuns went to the camp, where they found the little girl alone in the tent, "all painted and ready to start for the hills as soon as she would die." Outside the tipi a horse stood harnessed to a travois loaded with the child's playthings. Helpless to reverse the child's condition, the nuns joined the death vigil, then watched as the women of the clan wrapped the lifeless little body in canvas and placed it on the travois.

The sisters accompanied the sad procession across "ditches, fields, and forests" until the mourners finally stopped on a rocky hilltop, where the Indian women dug a hole about two feet deep, while others gathered poles and branches. The child's body was placed in the grave, together with all her favorite things. "Everything was then covered with a blanket," the sisters reported. Poles were laid across the grave, a second blanket was placed over the poles, and "stones and mud were

Left: A young frontier couple, Jeb and Sue Hanks, carved their baby's headstone on this river-smoothed boulder found near Brackett Creek in southwestern Montana.

piled on until they had formed a mound about four feet high." The Indians then began their "moaning cry," a lamentation kept up until sundown.[46]

Delia Klaus, the oldest of three girls, was nine when her mother died at the family home in western North Dakota. "That very night our dad and this good neighbor took . . . lumber and made our mother a coffin," Klaus recalled fifty years after the fact. "The ladies washed her, and with Dad's help they dressed her with the new clothes he had [just gone to town and] bought her, not knowing [they] would be her last." Early the next morning, Delia's father placed her mother's body on the wagon, hitched up his team, bundled up his three little girls, and crying "pitifully," set out for his parents' home some fifty miles away. After the funeral the three little girls stayed on with their grandparents while their father "returned . . . all by himself [to] the empty sod shack."[47]

The Plight of Orphans

Fortunately, the Klaus children had the support of their grandparents as well as their father after the death of their mother. Other children were not as fortunate, and orphanages—which also served half-orphans and children whose parents were still living but destitute—sprang up across the frontier during the latter half of the nineteenth century. Occupancy rates varied with circumstance, but most institu-

Above: *"Orphan train" children, newly arrived in Kansas from the East, ca. 1900, pose on the engine and cars of the Atchison, Topeka, and Santa Fe Railroad. Transported to rail centers across the state, they will be considered as possible wards by townspeople and farmers eager to help—or exploit—their young charges.*

Right: *A group of orphan train children and their escorts from the Children's Aid Society in New York City pose on their arrival in Lebanon, Missouri, on December 31, 1909. According to the Laclede Republican of January 7, 1910, "The children were exceptionally bright and attractive, ranging in age from 2½ years to 15 years," and all twelve were placed in homes in Laclede County.*

78

The Children of the Orphan Trains

Founded in 1853 in an attempt to "save" city urchins from the adverse influences of their environment, the Children's Aid Society moved some 150,000 homeless children from eastern metropolitan areas to rural towns, farms, and ranches of the West. For almost sevety-five years, the society's "orphan trains" rolled out of New York City and Boston, carrying their little passengers to Kansas, Missouri, Nebraska, Oklahoma, the Dakotas, and Montana.[a]

Charles Loring Brace, the society's founder, painted an idyllic picture of the operation: "[T]he ragged and dirty little ones," he wrote, "are gathered to a central office from the streets and lanes" of New York, then "cleaned and dressed, and sent away, under charge of an experienced agent." Upon their arrival in some rural village, "a great public meeting" was held and a citizens' committee was formed "to decide on the applications." Farmers came from within a twenty- to twenty-five-mile radius, looking for the "model boy [to]. . . . do the light work of the farm." Childless mothers came in hopes of replacing lost children. Housekeepers came in search of "girls to train up"; mechanics sought "boys for their trades." And, Brace concluded, "[I]n a few hours the little colony is placed in comfortable homes." If, by chance, problems arose, he said, "the committee replaces the children, or the agent revisits the village, while a steady correspondence is kept up by the central office with the employers."[b]

In actuality, the situation was not always so idyllic. While some "placed-out" children later spoke of having been "just tickled to have parents," others recalled hardships beyond those they had known on the streets of New York and Boston. For a boy sent to Kansas, arduous farm work was interspersed with beatings and threats of more physical violence if he did not pretend that all was well when the Aid Society agent came to call.[c]

"We were three days and two nights getting out to Nebraska," one of the orphan train children recalled in adulthood. "They took out the seats and put them back crossways to make beds. . . . We had milk and bread and red-jelly sandwiches three meals a day. . . To this day, I don't eat jelly." Margaret Braden, placed out as a four-year-old in South Dakota, recalled years later: "They put us all on a big platform . . . while people came from all around the countryside to pick out those of us they wished to take home." Some families were quite specific in their requests: "We asked for a boy of 18 months with brown hair and blue eyes and the bill was filled to the last specification," a Nebraska man reported.[d]

Boys were more frequently and more easily placed than girls, younger children were in more demand than older, and no blacks or foreign-born youngsters were brought into the program. Since there was no legal documentation concerning a child's placement—only a verbal agreement between the Aid Society's agent and the adult taking the child—employers could, and sometimes did, abandon children. A child needed as an extra hand in harvest season became an extra person to feed when winter set in, and some employers simply sent the children on their way. A parent in the East could also call a child home: A woman who was sent to a Nebraska home when she was nine years old, then returned to New York three years later at her father's request, wistfully recalled: "I had a nice room, good meals, taking lunch out to the men out in the fields. . . going to quilting parties, also County Fairs. . . . For three short years, I had love."[e]

By the 1920s, the professionalization of social services and a change in societal attitudes led to the demise of the Children's Aid Society and brought an end to the orphan trains.[f]

---

[a] Holt, *Orphan Trains*, 3; *Orphan Train Heritage Newsletter*, Fall 1987.

[b] Holt, 55.

[c] Holt, 78, 139.

[d] Holt, 59–60, 41, 119.

[e] Holt, 54, 140, 63, 130.

[f] Holt, 4.

Right: In this June 1894 photograph of the residents of St. Joseph's Orphanage in Helena, Montana, the little girls in the front row hold babies, not dolls. The newer arrivals are identified by their shaved heads, a widely prescribed preventive against lice infestations.

tions were filled to capacity. At times St. Vincent's Orphanage in Santa Fe, established in 1865 by the Sisters of Charity of Cincinnati, Ohio, housed as many as one hundred children.[48]

Before 1893, when the Montana legislature authorized the establishment of the Orphans Home in Twin Bridges, the destitute children and orphans of that state had been entirely reliant on religious institutions such as St. Joseph's Home in Helena. Even after the state orphanage was finally opened, St. Joseph's remained so crowded that children were "packed on the [dining hall] benches like peas in a pod."[49]

Opened in Butte in 1900, the Paul Clark Home was financed by William Clark, one of Montana's "Copper Kings," and named for his son, who had died in his late teens four years earlier. Envisioned as a haven for "the orphans and friendless" of the city, the home was "perfectly arranged and equipped" to accommodate as many as 150 children.

Housed in an elegant building, it had classrooms, dormitories, an infirmary, a "club room," a library and writing room, and a day nursery. "Industrial training" was provided for the residents. Girls were taught to sew and to do "the very finest class of laundry work"; boys received training in the trade "they desire[d] to follow." The home was run with such loving efficiency by the women of the Associated Charities that many children of Butte who lived within their own family circles were openly envious of the "advantages" enjoyed by the residents of the Paul Clark Home.[50]

"Born in between the last of eight boys" in San Francisco in 1897, Edith Pollock Schumacher had only "vague memories" of her father, who died when she was four, and "no recollection at all" of her mother, though an older brother told her that her mother had spent hours proudly brushing Edith's long black hair. He also told her

that her mother had never left her side from the moment she came down with spinal meningitis, praying "all the time that if God had to take a child of hers, he'd take one of her boys, and leave her her girl."

Then the mother herself took sick. "[She] was alive when they took us away," Edith was told, "but she was very ill. [She] went to the hospital and we went to the orphanage." There Edith's beautiful hair was shaved, and she and her brothers were put to work. Young as she was, Edith was expected to clean the dining room after breakfast, scrub hallway floors, and clean bathrooms. Before long, Edith fell in with her brother's plan to run away. He remembered where their house was, he told her, and they could live there together. Back in the family home, the two found a few pieces of stale bread, which her brother soaked in water, dipped in sugar, and shared with Edith. By the time the two had run out of bread, they had been discovered by neighbors, who dutifully notified the orphanage.

Though they were punished, the runaways were determined to try again. This time their escape route took them by a firehouse, where the firemen, recognizing them by their clothing as inmates of the orphanage, took them in, offering them chocolate and doughnuts. "Oh, my, we had a grand breakfast," Schumacher remembered. But before long the authorities arrived to take them back to the orphanage, where the truants finally accepted their fate. "We figured we'd have to make the best of what we had," Edith admitted, "so we stayed."[51]

Class Distinctions

Though their numbers were not great, affluent families also went west—or found their fortunes in the West—and the children of these households enjoyed a life of privilege that rivaled upper-class life in the East. In the early 1890s Helena, Montana, was said to be the richest city per capita in the United States. In this frontier settlement children of prominent families participated in activities that reflected the social whirl of eastern cities. Edna Hedges, daughter of a wealthy lawyer and politician, enjoyed tea parties, croquet, skits,

Above: The Montana State Orphans Home was opened in Twin Bridges in the mid-1890s, and in 1896 the children were gathered on the expansive grounds for this group portrait. Note the little girls in the center and left of center who have crossed the gender line to stand with their big brothers.

Right: Pictured with their parents at Fort Keogh, Montana, in April 1901, the Lindsley children, like most offspring of career army officers, grew up on various posts across the frontier.

Below: In 1868, Clarence Goodell, Henry Reed, and Albert Fisher, sons of affluent merchants and professionals in Helena, Montana Territory, enjoyed leisure activities markedly different from those of the average homesteader's child.

and parlor games with her friends and parents. Her father wrote Latin epigrams in her autograph album and took her for walks; her mother taught her the womanly arts and expected her to work at the traditional household tasks, "but not too hard."[52]

Daughters of a prosperous Helena merchant, Frieda and Belle Fligelman attended performances at the Ming Opera House and joined some twenty other children every Saturday afternoon for lessons at the Sulgrove Dancing Academy. "We learned the two-step and the waltz. . . and for special occasions we danced the minuet," Belle Fligelman Winestine recalled. "The boys had to wear a [single] white glove. . . . [for] each boy had to have his hand in the small of the girl's back and lest he get her dress soiled, he would have a white glove on. . . . And the other hand went straight out and kind of sawed the air as you went around."[53]

While the homesteaders' children hiked to nearby swimming holes and irrigation ditches, Frieda and Belle Fligelman were taken to the Broadwater Natatorium, where they donned long stockings and one-piece

Above: In 1870 the family of Don Vicente Lugo, a wealthy Californio, posed outside their impressive adobe home.

swimming suits that had "a big sailor collar" and "very full skirts that bubbled up with the water." In the evenings Herman Fligelman read to his daughters from *Alice in Wonderland, Les Miserables, Black Beauty,* and *King Lear.* Sitting in a chair on the other side of the gas lamp, their stepmother, Getty, did handwork and listened along with the girls.[54]

Like others of their class in nineteenth-century California, the sixteen children of Mariano and Francisca Vallejo lived a genteel lifestyle of "splendid idleness." Offspring of one of California's largest landowners, these children slept on beautifully trimmed and embroidered sheets and were ministered to by their own personal servants. Their mother had two servants for her own personal needs, four or five more to grind corn, and six or seven who worked in the kitchen. Other servants were "continually occupied in washing clothes of the children," while still others saw to the general housekeeping chores and "nearly a dozen . . . [were] charged to attend the sewing and spinning."[55]

The Vallejos claimed to treat their many servants as members of the family—standing as godparents to their children, seeing to the education of those children, and providing professional medical care when they fell ill. Perhaps these benefits helped offset relatively low wages. Reportedly, Indians herding the Vallejo cattle were seldom paid more than "two or three bullock hides per month or six dollars in goods."[56]

Class distinctions of this sort were equally apparent at Fort Berthold in western North Dakota. In the late 1860s, when Martha Gray, the only child of the post physician, received a wax doll one Christmas, news of the acquisition traveled quickly across the fort's compound. Soon Martha noticed a gathering of Sioux children outside her window, watching her play with a doll quite different from their own stuffed deerskin dolls and dolls they made from sticks and clay. Although several Indian fathers tried to barter buffalo skins and beaver pelts for the doll, Dr. Gray declined all offers, knowing Martha's pride in "Waxy."[57]

Above, left and right: *Both Standing Holy and her older brother Crow Foot enjoyed the status of "favored child" of Sitting Bull, the Lakota chief. Crow Foot died with his father in an 1890 shootout, and Standing Holy's story is lost to history.*

The Favored Child

Such a doll would have been the perfect gift for the "favored child" of the Native American culture. Usually a child of the tribe's wealthiest family, the *minipoka*, as the child was called by the Blackfeet, was pampered with praise and elaborate gifts— miniature tipi covers, toys, and fancy clothes. Such privilege bore responsibility, for these children grew up knowing that they would eventually be expected to assume important roles in the military or ceremonial life of the tribe.[58]

Sitting Bull, the Lakota chief, sired two favored children, a boy and a girl. At five years of age, young Crow Foot sat at council as his father surrendered to U.S. forces in July 1881, and it was Crow Foot who handed over Sitting Bull's rifle, the token of final surrender, to the commanding officer. Nine years later the boy was dead, having been killed, along with his father, in the shootout at Grand River, South Dakota. His twelve-year-old sister, Standing Holy, survived the day but disappeared from history.[59]

In the Hispanic culture the *consentido*, "the indulged son," was usually, but not always, the youngest boy, and this favored

Children of Mixed Parentage

If *minipoka* and *consentido* were coveted designations for "favored children," "half-breed" was a label to be feared and avoided. The offspring of white and Indian parents—most typically, a white father and an Indian mother—had no status with either culture. Such a child was, in a sense, orphaned in both worlds, white and Indian, although the census taker who applied the label "half-breed" invariably counted the child as Indian in his tabulation.[a]

However, not all children of mixed parentage suffered the scorn of society. Jean Baptiste Charbonneau, son of Toussaint Charbonneau, a French-Canadian trader, and Sacagawea, his sixteen-year-old Shoshone wife, was the "favored child" of a very special group of men. Born at Fort Mandan in North Dakota on February 11, 1805, Jean Baptiste was less than two months old when he joined his parents on the 4,000-mile jaunt known today as the Lewis and Clark Expedition. Dubbed "Pompey" or "Pomp" by William Clark, the infant spent sixteen months riding on his mother's back in a blanket shawl by day and falling to sleep at night in the buffalo-skin tipi that sheltered his parents and the expedition's leaders, Captains Lewis and Clark. The delight of the Corps of Discovery, little Pomp also served a strategic purpose for the men, for his presence helped reassure the natives they encountered that their mission was a peaceful one.[b]

---

[a] Albert Hurtado, "'Hardly a Farm House—A Kitchen without Them': Indian and White Households on the California Borderland Frontier in 1860," *Western Historical Quarterly* 13 (July 1982): 245–70, 268.

[b] James, *Notable American Women*, 3: 219; Gridley, *American Indian Women*, 48.

child was often given to his grandparents to be raised, presumably to be a comfort to them in age. Though not the youngest son in his family, Lorin Brown of Taos, New Mexico, had established a strong rapport with his grandmother at an early age, and so he was delighted to learn that he had been chosen *consentido*. From the day he was given to his grandparents, young Brown was "free as the wind, with all the streams and hills to roam, orchards to purloin."[60]

Among the Chinese, as among the Hispanics, boys were far more likely to be favored than girls, though there were so few women and children in the Chinatowns that sprang up throughout the West that one resident recalled that "[all] babies were looked on with a kind of wonder, . . . and infants and children were given special treatment by doting parents and many 'bachelor-uncles.'"[61]

"Special treatment" for girl babies included the perpetuation of the old-country ritual of foot-binding, and in 1883 a Nevada County (California) judge found a Chinese mother guilty of cruelty for binding the feet of her little girl "to make her more desirable for marriage." With time, however, acculturation began to affect Chinese communities. The 1900 census for Nevada County, for example, listed Euro-American given names for all nine children of a Chinese family.[62]

By the beginning of the twentieth century, the melting pot effect, as demonstrated by the cross-cultural naming of offspring, was in evidence all across the frontier. Indeed, even those children living in the relative isolation of a Chinatown or a rural homestead were being influenced by the ethic and expectations of a world beyond the family circle.

Opposite, above: A Montana logger's wife and child join him up Warm Springs Creek as he skids a giant log down to the mill in the winter of 1892.

Opposite, below: Reverend E. J. Stanley's family welcomes an unidentified preacher to their summer "camp meeting" grounds. The family's annual stay in the mountains featured many of the comforts of home, including the children's wagon and the baby's rocking high chair.

Blurred Boundaries

Frontier Children at Work and Play

For frontier children play often mimicked work, and work was sometimes carried out in the spirit of play. And though the specifics varied from culture to culture, the playtime activities of the children of the trans-Mississippi West were quite similar. The Cree child and the settler's child both rode stick horses. The Kawaiisu and the Chinese child both played tag and hide-and-seek. Hispanic children in Taos played a game called *gallinita ciega*, "little blind hen," and children in Skagway, Alaska, played "run sheep run." Girls on the plains, whether Native American or white, built playhouses out of buffalo bones and sagebrush twigs. The boys of the Kansas frontier, whether homesteader or Kaw, challenged each other to footraces. Both the Nootka and the Californio threw spears and stones at targets. And across the northern frontier children of all cultures skimmed across frozen ponds and rivers and slid down snow-covered hillsides.[1]

In all of these games were embedded elements of the roles these frontier children would assume as grown-ups, and as coordination, stamina, and strength increased, boys and girls alike set aside the toys of childhood and took up the tools of the adult world. For most children, this transition was fairly gradual, but for others, "play" never seemed an option since their very survival depended upon their learning to fend for themselves at an early age.

Indian Games and Chores

Native American children barely out of toddlerhood participated in games that developed physical endurance and strength, inuring them to the environment and schooling them in the lifeways of their people. With their parents, the children of the Plains Indians traveled under the harsh sun in midsummer and worked and played out of doors in winter. In 1821 frontiersman Jacob Fowler observed "more than one thousand" Indian children at play on the frozen Arkansas River of Colorado, engaging in "all kinds of sport" and "appear[ing] quite warm and . . . lively." Those who were too young to walk were "taken by the larger ones and set on a piece of skin on the ice, and in this situation the small one kick[ed] its legs and holler[ed] and laugh[ed] at those round it."[2]

Opposite: The Bartetto children of Crisman, Colorado, exhibit their skills with a crosscut saw, 1906. Summer chores for most frontier youngsters included helping to cut, split, and stack the family's supply of wood.

Left: Like their counterparts in other cultures, Indian children spent hours playing "house." Some little girls devised their own tipis out of materials at hand, but this Blackfoot girl has been gifted with an elaborate replica.

Top, left: *For an 1879 studio portrait with his little sister, this young Sioux chose to pose with the bow and arrow with which he was learning to stalk squirrels, rabbits, and other small game.*

Top, right: *Having learned to mother their dolls, young girls moved easily into the task of caring for younger siblings. In 1908 a photographer on the Pine Ridge (South Dakota) Reservation caught Marie tending to little At-a-la-ee.*

Below: *This 1851 pencil sketch captures a Kaposia youth's sweeping return of the ball in a game of lacrosse. According to artist Frank Blackwell Mayer, the "feathers, ribbons, streamers of red cloth" in the players' greased, combed, and plaited hair and the pendants of "feathers, furs & cloth" hanging from their breech cloths "contribute[d] greately to the effect of motion as they fl[ew] rather than r[a]n after the ball."*

Indian children juggled stones, made cat's cradles, played a version of jacks, and fashioned spinning tops from acorns. In addition, they, like their immigrant counterparts, engaged in playacting that prepared them for adult life. Little girls played "house" with toy tipis and carried deerskin dolls and puppies on their backs in little cradleboards. Little boys hunted birds and prairie dogs with half-sized bows and arrows and engaged in tugs-of-war and mock battles.[3]

Rough, aggressive play was encouraged by most tribes, and all games involved some form of competition. Apache boys engaged in shooting contests, marble games, and wrestling matches. They raided hives in yucca plants, pretending to fight the bees as they would an enemy and continuing to fight, even if stung, in order to prove their bravery to the adults looking on. Older Sioux boys played a fire-throwing game, the object of which was to cause the opponents to flee from the flaming clubs of one's team. Another hardy Sioux amusement was a game in which teams tried to kick their opponents into submission. "Some boys got badly hurt," Iron Shell, a Sioux elder, recalled. "But afterwards we would talk and laugh about it."[4]

Apache girls engaged in horse races and footraces, and Sioux girls played a form of field hockey. Cheyenne girls played a game similar to the game of hackeysack, keeping a leather ball stuffed with antelope hair aloft with their feet. Shell Flower, later known as Sarah Winnemucca, played with little animal figures and dolls made of clay; she painted faces on the inner bark of the juniper and created miniature villages with tiny lodges and cooking fires. In the spring she and other Northern Paiute girls made garlands of the flower for which each had been named, then danced and sang about that flower, becoming the flower itself for a brief afternoon.[5]

Delfina Cuero, a Kumeyaay from southern California, recalled running footraces, hunting rabbits, and jumping off high rocks to prove her bravery. She also played a game in which she and the other children threw gourds at one another. "Sometimes boys and girls would be on both teams and other times it would be boys against girls," she recalled.[6]

As Cuero and other girls grew older, they spent less time playing games and more time fashioning moccasins and ceremonial clothing and dressing and tanning hides. In due time make-believe chores gave way to real ones. From an early age a Sioux girl helped her mother wash cooking utensils, gather wood, and pick berries. By the time she was ten years old these tasks were hers alone. Girls as young as six were sometimes left in total charge of feeding, changing, and amusing a younger sibling.[7]

Boys, too, set aside their games in order to guard the camp, collect fuel, fetch water, and tend the horses. The youngest boys stalked squirrels, rabbits, turkeys, possums, and porcupines on foot. Older boys tested their skills farther from home, riding out on their ponies to hunt deer, antelope, elk, mountain sheep, and buffalo.[8]

Above: *The miniature wicker chairs and table, patterned cloth, and delicate china tea set—as well as the lace-trimmed blouses, matching striped frocks, and serious demeanor of these Minnesota sisters—depict a make-believe world that suggests the elegance and propriety of their 1880s urban home.*

Settlers' Children at Play

Like native children, most settlers' children were allowed a fair amount of playtime in which to pursue their own interests, but those interests did not go unnoticed by parents, most of whom had strong opinions as to appropriate play activities for boys and girls. As historian Elliott West has noted, boys were given "wooden horses, guns, tiny wagons, and lassos to fling at posts, dogs, chickens, and sisters," while girls often received gifts that suggested "an indoor future of domestic tasks." At the start of Adrietta Applegate's trip to Oregon with her family in 1851, she was given a reticule—a small bag filled with scraps of quilting, thread, and a thimble—on the assumption that she would amuse herself on the trip across the plains by learning to sew.[9]

Frontier Daughters and Their Dolls

Dolls were treasured toys for frontier girls of all cultures. When Martha Gray, nine-year-old daughter of the post physician at Fort Berthold in western North Dakota, received a wax doll one Christmas in the late 1860s, word spread quickly to the nearby Sioux encampment. Soon a group of little Indian girls was standing outside the Gray house, eager to have a look at "Waxy," the doll that was so different from their own stuffed deer-skin dolls.[a]

Daughters of wealthy families like the Grays sometimes owned entire collections of dolls. Seven-year-old Mary Margaret French and nine-year-old Bettina Bush, both daughters of doctors in Grand Forks, North Dakota, spent hours playing dolls together. Bettina's ten "children" lived in a special room of their own in the Bush household. Her oldest, twins Geraldine and Genevieve, were best friends with Dorothy, the oldest "child" in Mary Margaret's doll family. The two girls delighted in their "brilliant and adorable children" and wrote stories about them, exchanging new episodes by mail after Bettina and her family left Grand Forks.[b]

While girls from prosperous families played with delicate, hand-painted porcelain or wax dolls that had complete wardrobes, little cradles, and miniature dish sets, girls from less affluent families created dolls of wood or rags or cornhusks. Other little girls were even more creative in their doll play. When the hot summer days of the Montana plains sent Urma DeLong down into the root cellar to play, she entertained herself with a family of frogs that she diapered and dressed. "I [would] lay them down to put their diaper on," she recalled years later. "They just lay there and let me do it. When it got wet, I changed its little diaper—we always had chunks of outing flannel. . . . I had more fun with my little frogs!"[c]

Top, left: *A Cheyenne child and her doll in matching dress.*

Top, right: *Two Oregon girls hold a party for their family of dolls.*

Below: *Little Hilma Hanson of Butte, Montana, poses with her wax doll in this 1883 portrait. Dressed in dotted swiss over pink cambric, the doll was named Christina Nilsson—after a prominent Swedish singer.*

---

[a] Hampsten, *Settlers' Children*, 32.
[b] Hampsten, *Settlers' Children*, 28–29.
[c] West, "Child's Play," 12; Urma DeLong Taylor interview by Donna Gray, p. 77 in Linda Hasselstrom, Gaydell Collier, and Nancy Curtis, *Leaning into the Wind: Women Write from the Heart of the West* (Boston: Houghton Mifflin, 1997).

Similarly, little boys were encouraged to mimic their fathers' activities. Davy and George Christie, aged seven and five when they were brought to Montana Territory from Minnesota in 1885, used log scraps from their father's work on the family cabin to build a little house of their own—complete with a roof made of boards and buckskin.[10]

Stephanie Prepiora, who grew up on a farm near Minto, North Dakota, learned, like almost every homesteader's child, that a good imagination could fill playtime hours. "We were not over-indulged with toys and play gadgets," Prepiora recalled. "We used our imaginations and improvised." Though she owned a store-bought doll, the dollhouse and buggy she "built" for that doll were fashioned out of paper. Other than toys of their own devising, the only plaything the Lien children of central Montana had was a little red wagon their father brought home. "We had a lot of fun pulling that [wagon] around, picking up different rocks and things and putting them in it," Kaia Lien Cosgriff remembered.[11]

Above: *An Oregon girl sets the table for an 1859 tea party with her dog. The battered chair and packing-crate table, the dish-towel tablecloth and mismatched dishes mirror the make-do circumstances of frontier life.*

Left: *By 1910, with her mother busy with a new-born, young Leta Casey of Greybull, Wyoming, was already tending her siblings as well as her dolls. Upon her mother's death shortly after the birth of a fifth child, Leta's make-believe world came to an abrupt end as she assumed home-making and child-care duties for her father, who never remarried.*

Right: *Fueled by high-octane imaginations, this nail-keg tractor with its elaborate gearshift, smokestack, and levers transported these farm boys, their hay wagon, and their packing-box combine across the rolling prairies of western Minnesota in the summer of 1905.*

Right: *The Sweeney kids—Howard, Ambrose, George, and Mary—wanted their favorite horse in this 1919 photograph taken on the family's Fallon Flats (Montana) homestead.*

Horses and Ponies

The imaginative play of the Hispanic boys of Taos was based on their fascination with horses. "My peers and I knew every horse in the vicinity," Lorin Brown recalled, "from the saddle horses, to the harnessed ones . . . to those used by the freighters. It was no wonder that in our play we emulated horses. Cupping small milk cans in our hands, we lived on all fours for three or four years. We were the bucking bronc, the race horse, and the fancy gaited saddle horse." The boys' favorite was a stallion penned behind a board fence near the area where they played. "We would catch glimpses of his head and forefeet as he reared and snorted defiance toward any possible rival," Brown recalled. "Such power . . . thrilled us so that for days afterward we all were stallions, pawing the earth and shrilling defiant blasts to the world at large."[12]

Kaia and Sam Lien were enamored of horses from the moment they first caught sight of a large herd grazing "out in the hills" near their family's homestead on the Yellowstone River. To their amazement, the animals allowed themselves to be petted and talked to. The morning after this marvelous discovery, Kaia removed the drawstrings from her petticoat and fashioned them into a "rope," telling Sam, "Now we can go out and get our horse." Back at the pasture, she made good her promise, looping the string around the neck of a horse and leading it home. "Mama," Kaia called into the cabin, "come and see what we've got." Incredulous, their mother asked, "What is that?" "It's a horse," Kaia said with pride. "Well, take it back where you got it," her mother said, turning back to her work. "And that, Kaia recalled, "was the last of that episode."[13]

All four little Rietzes of Rock Creek, Wyoming, would regularly mount their father's Indian pony, Midnight, and set off on a bareback ride that was inevitably brief. After little more than a mile, Minnie Rietz recalled, Midnight would simply "put his head between his knees and raise his hind quarters high enough to send us all scooting over his head. . . . [then] race for home, leaving us to walk in. . . . [W]e never did [get the best of him.]"[14]

Farmyard Pets

Children who had no horse to ride often managed to harness dogs, goats, even turkeys, to homemade or store-bought carts or wagons for fun at home or in parades. "The things that would please a child then," Montana pioneer Urma DeLong Taylor observed, "they wouldn't even think of [playing with] today."[15]

Above: Clutching a tiny doll and a half-grown cat, Frances Ashbridge sends her older sister, Hazel, skyward on a twenty-foot teeter-totter made from a sturdy plank borrowed from a lumber pile on the family's sheep ranch in central Montana.

Above: Foster Tusler astride the family's pet sow, eastern Montana, 1902.

The "pleasures" of newly arrived farm-yard pets are evident in an 1860 letter from twelve-year-old Mary Rebecca Williams of Homer, Iowa, to her older brother James, who was working in Augusta, Georgia. "I will tell you our calves names," Becky wrote. "[T]he largest is Marmy Duk[e]. Curly. Prince Albert. Queen Victoria. Princes Adalade. Hatty. Cupid. . . . [O]ld Brunts calf [we call] Moon, because he has such big eyes."[17]

When Martha Gay of Greene County, Missouri, brought home a "bum" lamb she had found on her way to school, she was overjoyed to be told she could keep the abandoned animal as a pet. The lamb thrived under her care and was soon following her around the farm and occasionally accompanying her to school. "We . . . had many a romp with our lamb," she remembered in later years. However, as "Billy" grew from lambdom into ramdom, problems developed. One day when Martha was tending her baby brother, Billy attacked the child. Though Martha managed to intervene, the baby was injured "quite

Stephanie Prepiora and her brothers and sisters always looked forward to spring and the arrival of new colts and calves on their North Dakota homestead. "How we would pet them and spoil them," Prepiora recalled. "There were baby chicks, turkeys, ducks and geese, all requiring work but it was a work of love and all pleasures."[16]

Right: The care and feeding of the spring 1904 crop of "bum" lambs on the Nelson ranch in Wyoming fell to this young lad and his sister. Nurturing lambs abandoned by their mothers took patience and persistence, and even with excellent care, orphaned lambs did not always survive.

Above: *By 1900 affluent children in Helena, Montana, were participating in such culturally enriching activities as this costume ball at Sulgrove's Dancing Academy.*

badly." Soon thereafter, Billy was taken to market, and his young owner was "not sorry to see him go."[18]

Urma DeLong Taylor, who grew up on the plains of eastern Montana, adopted a baby chick she had found hobbled by a tangle of horsehair that had wound itself around his little feet. "Pete" quickly became a "spoiled child" who "lived right in the house" and even "perched . . . on the edge [of the sugar bowl]." The full-grown chickens that scratched about the barnyard of their family's Wyoming ranch served as "doggies" on which Charline Sackett and her brother practiced their calf-roping skills. Donning oversized hats, they mounted their stick horses and went about the business of roping, throwing, and branding their flock of chickens. One "particularly cross old cock" always presented a challenge, keeping the game interesting long after the more subservient fowl had been duly caught and "branded."[19]

Indoor Amusements

When play moved indoors, children got out sets of dominoes, made shadow pictures on walls, and created entertainments for one another. "[We] used to put on shows," Ann Skocilich Pentilla of Butte, remembered. "The kids would make up shows and go to an old barn and put on shows and charge a nickel or a dime." Some children were fortunate enough to live in frontier towns that boasted a movie theater. In Kemmerer, Wyoming, Iona Piper and her friends trooped to the Lyceum Theater, where a stereopticon threw colored pictures on the screen. Frequently a part of the program was an illustrated song presented by local musicians. "Silver Threads among the Gold," "The Old Oaken Bucket," and "Darling Nellie Grey" became the children's favorites.[20]

Mormon children enjoyed singing and dancing, and Brigham Young, the prophet who led the Saints to Zion, encouraged the development of theatrical talents in the

Excerpted entries from the diary of Inez Reichman, a preadolescent in Sedan, Montana:

AUG. 26 [1902], TUESDAY. Papa has brought a load of hay in this morning. Papa started back to the ranch just as quick after diner this after noon as he could. Finished the library book Robinson Croesoe. I took it down and had it . . . changed for Rudder Grange Dairy. Made the cherry jam today too.

SEPT. 2, TUESDAY We finished my sunbonnet and fixed Daisy's [Inez's older sister] gray skirt. We also finished the library book "That Girl Montana" and took it back and got "An Old fashioned Boy." The High school began today.

MONDAY, 22 SEPT. Papa went to the ranch. Began house cleaning. Got a letter from Kate. Answered Mrs. Petterson's letter.

THUR. [OCT] 9 Josie came over this morning and we went over there for dinner and spent the afternoon. We had a real nice dinner. One thing we had was apple dumplings. I started to make a quilt.

MON [OCT] 20 School began today. I took 1 doz eggs to Mrs Greenblatt. They gave me 50c Began to clean our bedroom. Mamma and Daisy went down town.

TUES., 21 Ivy came up and we run the town over from one end to the other. We got our pictures taken. Josie and Daisy went down town and Josie got a library book.

WED. OCT. 22 Mamma went down town and saw Mrs. Root take an exray treatment. We finished the bedroom. Got a box of apples.

Above: *Still too young to unravel the mysteries of the printed word, this Oregon lass "reads" the pictures and letters of a 1910 newpaper.*

young people of the church. Part of his plan for the development of Salt Lake City was the construction of a theater, and he and his wives and children could often be seen looking down on plays or pageants from a series of boxes perpetually reserved for their use.[21]

Some frontier youngsters, like children everywhere, were faithful to their diaries. The youngest in a family of five children living in Sedan, Montana, Inez Reichman used the quiet hours of the evening to record her day's activities. In the diary that survives, she wrote of selling her mother's eggs, milk, and cream to friends and neighbors, of visitors who came for dinner, of letters she had written and received, of books she was reading, and of attending church and Sunday school. Though she recorded no major life events—except for a serious illness—during the nine months covered by the diary, her entries, from the summer of 1902 to the spring of 1903, convey the flow of the life of a typical western child.[22]

And children read. "We used to go [to the Helena Public Library] quite often and bring home books," Belle Fligelman Winestine recalled. "It was the Elsie Dinsmore books that we cried over and Mother said she didn't want us to cry over books. That we would have to get different kinds of books. . . . But we kept on bringing home the Elsie books, and she would hide them from us." While the Fligelman girls were clandestinely reading the Elsie Dinsmore series, young Anne Ellis of Bonanza, Colorado, spent many an evening reading *Peck's Bad Boy* with Lil, one of the "notorious" women of the camp.[23]

Exploration and Adventure

Interactions between children and adults of less than stellar reputation were not uncommon, since children tended to ex-

in Frontier Montana

SAT. [FEBRUARY] 14 [1903]   I began working for Mrs. Spratt while she has the grip. I began at 11 o'clock a.m. and came home at 5:45 o'clock p.m. and intend to go back in the morning.

SAT [MARCH] 28   Daisy is sick.

FRI. [APRIL] 3   We washed. Well, I guess we are in for it for a while. The Dr. said Daisy had the Small Pox and has vaccanated and quarentined us.

SAT. 4   Well it will just be the same from now on for a while I guess—stayed in the yard and Dr. Leard came.

SUN. 5   Colored easter eggs. We were afraid we wouldn't be able by easter. Mamma set a hen. Dr. Beeson came.

SAT. 18   We were about to get out but they think I have the small pox so we will wait a few days.

WED. 22   They have decided this is only caused by the vaccination and are starting to fumigate. Daisy got out and went to Josie's because they didn't finish fumigating and Daisy is cleaned up and must not stay in the unfumigated house.

THUR. 23   They finished the house (fumigating) so we are free at last.[a]

---

[a] Reichman Family Papers, Montana State University Libraries.

plore all aspects of their environment. For the children of the railroad town of Kemmerer, Wyoming, the yard's turntable became a giant merry-go-round, and youngsters clambered up and slid down the face of the huge snowplow that sat idle during the summer months. They also climbed aboard the sidetracked cars at will, playing engineer or fireman or conductor for days on end. The children of Butte, Cripple Creek, and other mining towns played on slag heaps and made mud pies from the dusty residue of the extraction operations.[24]

Every Thursday during the summer months, the children of Butte were given free admittance to Columbia Gardens, that city's early-day version of a theme park. A gift to the town from Copper King William Clark, the Gardens were a child's delight, boasting a Ferris wheel, a roller coaster, a carousel, and well-kept picnic

Above: *Firearms, instruments, and flag at the ready, members of this 1899 Sonora, California, fife-and-drum corps enjoy their own brand of cultural enrichment.*

grounds. On Thursdays, youngsters also got a free round-trip ride on the streetcar, or "dinky," that took them from the center of town out to the Gardens.[25]

When Columbia Gardens closed for the season, the children of Butte turned to winter sports, flying down the city's steep hills on homemade toboggans that held up to sixteen riders or "sluicing" the slopes on barrel-stave skis. "All the broken ankles . . .," one native mused. "But we . . . got by with it." It could take as long as two hours to pull a toboggan up Anaconda Road, but the thrilling five-minute ride down the two-mile slope was always worth the effort. Just to the north of Butte, in Helena, children used the Lawrence Street hill for their ski and sled runs, flying through the streetcar crossing at the intersection of Lawrence and Benton. "I don't know how our parents ever trusted . . . that we wouldn't get run over," Belle Fligelman Winestine recalled years later.[26]

Above: Children of the mining frontier spent hours climbing about on abandoned machinery and structures. In this 1908 photo a brother and sister pose on an elevated sluice.

Right: The boys of Wendling, Oregon, a mill town, enjoyed playing with each other—and with their dogs.

Left: On Thursdays the children of Butte were given free trolley rides and admission to Columbia Gardens, the amusement park built by William Clark, one of Montana's fabled "Copper Kings."

Below: These children skiing in Yellowstone National Park in 1894 had that winter wonderland all to themselves.

Above: On a spring day in 1913, Geneva Fornell of LeRoy, Montana, fills her family's water barrel, a task she assumed as soon as she was old enough to drive the wagon.

Below: Gathering cow chips for fuel was a daily chore for these Nebraska brothers.

Rural Children at Work

Most settlers of the American West, whether prosperous or impoverished, thought of work as having value in and of itself, and most homesteaders' children were put to work soon after toddlerhood. As historian Elliott West has noted, children all across America were working, but "those on the frontier toiled at a greater variety of jobs."[27]

The tasks that fell to children were endless—and essential. Until a homestead had a well, water had to be hauled from the nearest source—a spring or creek. Children quickly learned it was easier to carry two buckets of water, one in each hand, than to struggle along, unbalanced, with only one. Some children trudged from creek to kitchen wearing a leather yoke from which dangled a pair of water pails. Matilda Peitzke Paul recalled, "I often had to get water from a spring and carry it out to the field for drinking for the workers before I was old enough to do other field work."[28]

On washdays children stood for long hours using a stick to poke down the clothes in the washpot of boiling water. They were often the ones charged with such tasks as emptying the slop jars each morning, collecting fuel for cooking and heating, chopping and stacking firewood, and trimming the wicks of kerosene lamps.[29]

Some jobs were just plain boring. Stephanie Prepiora's first assigned job was moving the cows on her family's North Dakota farm to pasture each morning, then keeping an eye on them as they grazed. "What a bore waiting for a cow to fill its enormous stomach," she remembered, "even the dog . . . would get bored and run home." Bessie Felton Wilson and her brother, Bernard, who grew up in Kansas in the 1870s, were also quickly bored with their assigned task of herding the family's pigs from field to field. To fill the hours, they gave names to the pigs and made up stories about them. "I used to make my brother believe that they were talking [to me] when they grunted," Wilson recalled, "and I being able to understand their hog latin would interpret to him."[30]

When the job of taking the cows to pasture was assigned to a younger sibling, Stephanie Prepiora took on other chores. She "milked the cows, helped clean the barn and chicken coop, [and] fed animals and poultry." Twelve-year-old Mary

Rebecca Williams of Homer, Iowa, and her nine-year-old brother, George, handled a similar variety of chores. "[We would] get up about six o'clock, eat our breakfast, then help to milk, get ready and go to school. Then about four in the evening run home, and if you were passing about that time you would see a little boy and a girl with spy glass in hand mounting the house top [to] look over the prairie's to see which way the cow's were." Having spotted the herd, the two would climb down from the roof and set out after them, "return[ing] about sundown with a drove of cattle."[31]

Although the three little Schumacher boys were aged only three to seven in 1888 when they arrived from Chicago in Stutsman County, North Dakota, they did the work of much older children. Whenever the well went dry—a common occurrence in that arid region—the boys drove the family's cattle to a neighboring farm for water. They were almost a quarter mile from home on one such trip when one of them realized that little Alfred, not quite two, had been following them. Arthur, the oldest, pointed the toddler toward home, and the brothers continued on their way, giving him no further thought. Not until her older boys showed up at home and asked about Alfred did Emilie Schumacher even realize that her youngest son was missing. After a frantic search, she and the boys finally discovered Alfred sound asleep on a soft badger mound.[32]

Nontraditional Roles

As the Schumacher boys grew stronger, they were required to take their turns pumping water from a basement cistern into the kitchen—a hundred strokes every day for each child. Their chores around the house and yard—in which they were eventually joined by tag-along Alfred and little sister Clara—also included gathering eggs, tending chickens and pigs, milking, separating cream, churning butter, and rendering lard. There were no gender distinctions made in assigning these chores.[33]

Above: On a brisk spring day in 1907, the Anderson children of Niwot, Colorado, scatter feed to the chickens, one of the first outdoor tasks assigned to fledgling farmhands.

Left: This child of Nebraska homesteaders took pride in being entrusted with the care of the spring's first calf.

Above: Emory Maury, center, helps put a new roof on a peg-construction homesteader cabin that, by 1910, was being used as an outbuilding on his family's Fergus County (Montana) ranch.

Below, left: A young man proudly shows off the row cultivator used on his family's ranch in Wyoming.

Below, right: A boy with a shotgun and a hunting dog was a common sight in turn-of-the-century Oregon, where frontier youngsters did their part to put game on the table.

"There were nine children in our family," Margaret Mitchell Womer of Kansas recalled, "Six girls and three boys, and as the girls were older and my father not strong, the hard toil . . . fell to the . . . girls. We used to set traps on the banks of the Republican [River] and caught wolves, badgers, bobcats and skunks." No gender distinctions were made in the chores assigned in the Callaway family of Virginia City, Montana, either. Llewellyn Callaway, who grew up to become the chief justice of the Montana Supreme Court, recalled that "the irksome tasks" of his boyhood included "getting the wood, . . . washing dishes, washing diapers, ironing and wheeling the baby carriage when I wasn't in school."[34]

Just into his teen years when his family moved to western Kansas in 1877, John Norton helped build and grout his family's dugout and plow and plant a large garden. He herded and hayed, planted and harrowed, and helped his mother sweep and scrub the floors, wash clothes, and cook. Stephanie Prepiora not only milked cows and tended livestock and poultry on the family's North Dakota homestead but also "[baled] and stacked hay, shocked grain, helped with the plowing, [and] helped with the housework and cooking."[35]

Born in Kansas in 1868, Mary Alice Zimmerman, who by her own report "was strong for a girl," regularly helped her father with heavy farm chores. "I soon preferred to have a team to myself when possible," Zimmerman recalled. "I have always loved the great open out-of-doors, and I think that it was as much from choice as from necessity that I was much of the time out on the farm at work with father."[36]

Oklahoma pioneer Susie Crocket would have welcomed those outdoor chores. "I hated to see Ma come in with a big batch of sewing," Crocket recalled, "for I knew it meant many long hours sitting by her side sewing seams." The system was unfair, she concluded: "I could help the boys with the plowing or trapping, but they would never help me with the sewing." Anne Fletcher of Glendive, Montana, did not have to complain about being kept to her sewing. She "worked in the hayfield from the time [she] was 13" and resented all the while being "thrown right out into . . . being a hired man" because of her father's death.[37]

Fieldwork could be a back-breaking task for a youngster. "I have plowed acre after acre from the time I was twelve years old," Percy Ebbut of Kansas remembered. The initial breaking of the sod, woven thick with the roots of grasses, took strength, even after the steel-tipped plow was introduced on the plains. "The soil was virgin," noted Mary Alice Zimmerman, who worked alongside her father on a Kansas homestead. "It had to be broken, turned, stirred, and taught to produce." After plowing his fields, one Oklahoma farmer gave his three children butcher knives, then he and his wife each took up an axe and the family began the arduous work of breaking up the clods.[38]

Breaking the soil was only one of many field chores done by settlers' children.

Above: *A brother and sister enjoy a hearty outdoor breakfast before they begin their share of the daily sheepherdering activities at a base camp in the Big Horn Mountains outside Ten Sleep, Wyoming, an area that would soon be embroiled in a vicious war between sheep ranchers and cattlemen.*

Below: *As this 1908 scene on a Montana homestead attests, dishwashing on the frontier was not reserved for women and girls.*

Right: After a morning's hunt on the open range of Wyoming, young Helen Irving mimics her mentors, Katherine and Frances Roberts, by displaying her gopher alongside their jack rabbits.

Right: An afternoon of creekside fishing with a willow pole and night crawlers yielded ten fish for this young Oregonian. Though too small by the standards of most adult anglers, these fish will likely soon grace the family's dinner platter.

Matilda Peitzke Paul, child of an Iowa homestead, remembered that once the field was planted and the seeds began to sprout, she and her brothers and sisters "had to stay out in the field and chase black-birds" to keep them from digging up the seed corn or eating the young sprouts. In the spring, she and her siblings were assigned the task of "pull[ing] weeds for the hogs for feed." They watched the family's cattle "to keep them out of other peoples as well as out of our own fields," and before she was old enough to bind grain, she helped to "carry bundles in piles, ready to be shocked up."[39]

"The Good Fun of Good Work"

Hamlin Garland, who chronicled a childhood on the plains in several autobiographical works, wrote of the "sordid monotony of farm life," but, as one scholar has noted, many memoirs convey "the good fun of good work." In west Texas, Ralla Banta wrote of her sheepherding days, "When we returned home in the evening, we enjoyed telling where we had been, to

Nebr. Lassie

By S D Butcher Kearney Neb.

what creek, up what branch, and what we had seen."[40]

Hunting was one chore children generally looked forward to. Rabbit hunting on Sundays was "about the only good time that we ever had," Dora Bryant remembered of her Oklahoma girlhood. "Compared with [hunting], everything else was as dust in the cyclone," Frank Waugh recalled of his childhood on the plains of Kansas.[41]

Children as young as seven or eight stalked and killed antelope, raccoons, ducks, geese, deer, prairie chickens, wild hogs, and rabbits. Martha Gay, whose early years were spent in western Missouri, was only four when she and her six-year-old brother, Martin, set their first traps and caught "birds and rabbits and carried them proudly home." When eleven-year-old Lee Whipple-Haslam's father was killed in a California gold camp, she took up the hunting that provided meat for the table of her mother's boardinghouse.[42]

Children on horseback found it easy to bridge the worlds of work and play. While

tending cows or sheep, they raced their ponies, practiced stunts, and chased coyotes and antelope. "It has been a novel sight," noted an observer newly arrived in northern Nebraska in the early 1880s, "to watch a little girl about ten years old herding sheep . . ., handling her pony with a masterly hand, galloping around the herd if they begin to scatter out, and driving them into a corral."[43]

Ursula Camastral, a ten-year-old immigrant from Switzerland, learned to ride a horse soon after arriving at the family's new homestead on the Judith River in central Montana. Because her mother thought it "very bad . . . for a girl or woman to ride straddle," Ursula was constrained to ride sidesaddle anytime she was near home. But her father allowed her to ride astride when she helped him round up wild horses, and she quickly gained a reputation as a skilled horsewoman.[44]

Rural Work for Hire

Sometimes the work of children brought in cash for the family. The milking and

Above: Although obviously a novice, young Alice Butcher obliges her uncle, Nebraska photographer Solomon D. Butcher, by trying her hand at a chore regularly practiced by many frontier children

Right: With spreads like the Big Red Ranch in northeastern Wyoming paying bounties for the hides of wolves, coyotes, and other predators, many young people joined their elders in setting traps and skinning out their catch. In this 1898 photo a monkey sipping water from a tin cup sits atop the boy's stack of hides.

churning done by youngsters not only provided for their own nutrition but also gave the family butter and cheese to sell. Although he knew the importance of his work, Carl Jones of Merino, Wyoming, hated milking on winter mornings. To keep his bare feet warm, he would prod the cow to her feet, then plant his own feet on the spot where she had lain, the warmest spot in the barn.[45]

Nine-year-old Cliff Newland of west Texas hauled supplies to cowboys in line camps, a round trip of seventy-five miles. The fifty cents a day he earned helped support himself and his widowed father, who worked a small ranch. Fourteen-year-old John Norton brought in extra cash by selling the rabbits he killed and the bleached buffalo bones he and his siblings gathered near his family's homestead in western Kansas.[46]

Every week young Lorin Brown and three enterprising friends set out traps on a stream south of Taos. On Saturday mornings they gathered their harvest, then spent the afternoon "skinning [the] catch, fleshing the pelts, and [setting] them on willow stretchers to dry" until they were ready to be taken into town to be shipped to "a fur and pelt house in Denver."[47]

Fourteen-year-old Magdalena Martin and her eleven-year-old brother, John, were indentured by their father to a farmer who wanted them to pull his thresher, having heard that they had served as their father's draft animals in hauling stones for the foundation of a shed on their homestead near Ashley, North Dakota. In return for their labors, the farmer promised to buy each child a pair of shoes for the winter. Working and living conditions on the man's farm were intolerable—even for children who had known life in a boxcar during their first year in this country—and had Lena and John only known the way home, they would have escaped their horrible situation. They were saved only when their mother, who had never agreed to the bargain, persuaded their father to "steal" them home one Sunday while the farmer and his wife were at church.[48]

Irene Albro of Lane County, Oregon, helped support the family homestead by working in the hop fields with her mother and sisters every fall. Taking their tent and their "eats," they camped at the fields

Left: These boys of eastern Oregon, with ox yoked to stoneboat, are ready to begin the day's work.

south of Eugene for ten days, or until the crop was in. "Hop picking was hard work," Albro recalled. "We didn't make much money was the trouble of it." Hispanic children, who traditionally joined their parents as migrant farmworkers, also knew lean rewards for hard work.[49]

When pocket gophers became so thick in Albany County, Wyoming, in 1888 that they threatened crops and their holes

Below: Children from three families made up this 1910 crew of prune pickers near Riddle, Oregon.

Above: Children are much in evidence at this turn-of-the-century camp for migrant agricultural workers in southern California. Hispanic families, often seasonal immigrants from Mexico, moved as a unit and worked the fields together, with the children's labor adding to their parents' income.

threatened the footing of horses and cattle, children were paid five cents for each gopher scalp they brought in. Minnie Rietz was able to bring in her bounty by keeping an eye on her cat. Whenever that skilled hunter appeared with one of the rodents, Minnie coaxed the catch from her. At first the cat resented sharing her kill, but she soon learned that her dinner would be returned, once Minnie had taken the scalp.[50]

Urban Wage Earners

Children in mining camps and in boomtowns were set to work as frequently as were farm children. Mining companies often hired young boys to work at the "picking table" where coal was separated from stone and slate. Boys were also sent underground, where they worked twelve to fourteen hours a day, six days a week, in dark, poorly ventilated pits deep in the earth.[51]

Many of the boys and girls of Butte, Montana, were encouraged by their parents to go out into the streets in pursuit of fuel for the family stove. "The coal cars would run back and forth on Anaconda Road," Catherine Hoy recalled. "One kid would get in the coal car and throw out all this coal. Then the rest of us would go along and pick it up and take it home." It was a dangerous pastime; at times children "fell between the cars and [were] killed." Children were also sent out to the mine entrances to fetch home the scraps of wood left there after the shafts had been built. Another child of Butte, Ann Skocilich and her siblings were assigned the summer job of chopping and sawing wood gathered for the winter. "My dad would haul in this old wood from the smelter and we would have to saw it and chop it and pile it," she recalled. "That was our vacation."[52]

The work of other youngsters brought in cash for their families. San Francisco journalist Elodie Hogan described the various little peddlers who haunted that city's streets in the early 1890s, beginning with the newsboy, "a clamorous, ubiquitous sprite, untidy, nimble, cunning, coming always with a halo of ringing din around him." Working his route along sidewalks and in the middle of streets, the newsboy "risk[ed] his neck and bones in getting . . . [on and off] moving [cable] cars." Waving his papers in the faces of potential custom-

Left: In 1893, California Illustrated carried these woodcuts of children at work on the streets of San Francisco: a boy stashes bits of coal into a gunnysack, and a girl from the North Beach section of the city carries home wood she has gathered for the family stove.

ers, he often made a sale "from sheer force of personal magnetism." The newsboy was a veritable "thesaurus on legs," Hogan concluded, but she found it "appalling and bewildering to hear the joyous trebles of these small human entities piping murder, war, fire and explosions."[53]

Elodie Hogan was equally intrigued with the city's match boys, whom she described as "a tribe of philosophers in small breeches whose . . . . complete stock in trade consists of four dozen bunches of matches swung over his shoulders in a calico bag, a good pair of legs to pack him, and a solemn air of unconcern as to the general wagging of the world." The four dozen bunches of matches could net thirty-five cents, but Hogan noted the disadvantage under which match boys labored, since "Their business takes them toward the kitchen where nickels are scarce, not out on the thoroughfares where loose change flows free."[54]

Fruit hawkers, fishmongers, flower peddlers—all underage— plied their wares on the streets and docks of San Francisco. Very small boys, often as young as six, sold gum and newspapers outside the houses of the tenderloin district in the early hours of the morning. Ten-year-old girls worked in pickle

factories. On the street, boys followed drunks, pleading for money and waiting for the opportunity to roll their victims.[55]

Children as young as seven worked in canneries, where their hands became drawn and crippled with cuts from paring knives. "The acid of the fruits [ate] the tender flesh to the bone," a San Francisco paper reported. "More than fifty . . . children [crippled in this manner] could be found at one school," the article claimed. In 1905, when the California legislature passed a law that banned the employment of any child under the age of fourteen "except during the regular vacations of the public schools," the law drew objections from not only employers but also parents who found they could no longer legally keep their offspring out of school to work in the canneries, to clerk in stores, or to drive delivery wagons.[56]

Not all children sought income-producing jobs at their parents' behest. Twelve-year-old Mollie Sheehan found innovative ways of earning her own spending money in Virginia City, Montana Territory, where her parents ran a boardinghouse. Mollie and her friend Carrie Crane would wait until the miners went home to their cabins after a day's work, then crawl into the sluice

Children on Strike

In 1903 business and social leaders of Butte, Montana, founded the Butte Newsboys Club to provide social and educational activities for the boys who peddled papers on the city's street corners. The activities, usually scheduled for evenings and weekends, included lectures, music, and picnics. The club also represented the boys in their business affairs with local newspapers.

In July of 1913 the newsboys agreed to buy copies of the *Butte Daily Post*, an afternoon paper, at two copies for five cents, five copies for ten cents, or thirteen copies for twenty-five cents—all to be retailed at five cents each. When the *Post* subsequently lowered subscription prices below these wholesale rates, the club stepped in on behalf of the newsboys and attempted to begin negotiations with the paper.

But on January 5, 1914, before talks were even begun, a strike erupted. On that afternoon the newsboys had gathered at the office of the *Post* on West Granite to press for new rates. When they discovered that the carriers who ran the subscription routes did not intend to join their protest and were, indeed, beginning their afternoon deliveries, the dissident newsboys attacked them and destroyed their papers. The young strikers then carried their cause to the streets, seizing papers from the vendors who were still working, from any carriers they came across, and even from customers. City police eventually acted to clear the area around the newspaper office, and plainclothes officers patrolled the *Post* building throughout the evening hours.

On the second day of the strike the newsboys marched through uptown Butte with banners supplied by the Industrial Workers of the World (IWW), a militant labor organization. "An injury to one is an injury to all," and "Direct action gets the goods," the banners proclaimed. That afternoon the boys were back at the *Post* building and out on the streets, where they seized more papers from carriers and customers.

At a special meeting that evening club members listened as their own leaders and several prominent citizens called for restraint and negotiation. By a vote of 58 to 30 the boys agreed to return to work and "to condemn those who had caused the violence and destruction." Although some boys vowed to continue their protest, sales of the *Daily Post* resumed without disturbance on January 7, and the Butte Newsboy Club was soon engaged in its more prosaic social activities.

The newsboys' strike was virtually ignored by the local press—aside from a notice in the *Post* itself declaring that the boys had broken their agreement and had engaged in destructive behavior. The *Butte Miner* buried news of the strike on its back pages and used its editorial page to denounce the boys' actions and to imply that the youngsters had been unduly influenced by the radical IWW.[a]

---

[a] Dale Martin, "School for Struggle: The Butte Newsboys Strikes of 1914 and 1919," *Speculator* 2 (Summer 1985): 9–11.

boxes and scrape the bottoms and sides with their hair brushes, gathering up the gold residue. Taking their gleanings home, they would dry the fine dust in the oven and blow the black sand from it.

"Sometimes we would find that our gold dust weighed to the amount of a dollar or more," Mollie Sheehan Ronan wrote in her memoir. "A man would have entered a sluice box not his own at risk of being shot on sight, but it amused the miners to have us little girls clean up after them. We were given so much encouragement that we actually thought we honored the men whose sluice boxes we chose to clean." However, their success at this new business was rela-

tively short-lived, since Mollie's father objected to—and ultimately forbade—her expeditions to the sluice boxes.[57]

Undaunted, Mollie began another business venture, in which the owners of the boomtown's boardinghouses and hotels paid her and her friends twenty-five cents in gold dust for bouquets of wildflowers with which to decorate their tables. From flowers the girls branched out into fresh vegetables. Since there was little fresh produce to be had in Virginia City in the spring of 1864, the first spring of the gold camp's existence, the girls went out into the fields and gathered lamb's-quarter, an edible weed when young and tender, and a fitting substitute for spinach. For "a gallon bucket crammed full" of lamb's-quarter, the girls received $1.50 in gold dust. "My career as a marketer of fresh flowers and 'greens' lasted only until my father learned what I was doing," Ronan recalled. "Saying that he would not have a daughter of his running about the streets and into hotels and public places," he quickly "put a stop to it," though her "gentle little stepmother" never objected to her "flitting about as free as a bird."[58]

Mollie Sheehan's enjoyment of her various business ventures stemmed, in large part, from the fact that her entrepreneurial endeavors were of her own devising and her job evolved from her unending fascination with Virginia City and its citizens. For most frontier children the best educational experiences, as well as the best work experiences, were those that engaged their imaginations and capitalized on their inherent curiosity about the world in which they lived.

Left: A child of Italian immigrants hauls water for railroad workers in the Wind River canyon of Wyoming, 1909.

Below: Quong Pock Huie (on the left), young son of Huie Pock, physician and surgeon, worked in his father's mercantile on the edge of Butte's flourishing Chinatown at the turn of the century. The store also served as the doctor's office.

All the World's a School

The Education of Frontier Children

By the middle of the nineteenth century most American children living in eastern towns and cities attended school on a fairly regular basis, but the educational experiences of children in the trans-Mississippi West were far less likely to take place in a formal setting. Indeed, until the federal government and various religious groups altered age-old customs, Native American children were educated through storytelling and imitation, through games and competitions, and through instruction by kin or tribal elders.

Though patterned after educational systems back east, the formal education of settlers' children could be a rather haphazard affair. The movement of families into a frontier settlement usually prompted the organization of a school, but on a local scale, that institution had humble beginnings. A boxcar, a sheep wagon, or a tent might be pressed into service as a classroom, and the nature and number of school sessions varied according to the availability and abilities of teachers, the labor constraints of the farming cycle, and the community's attitude toward education.

As a rule, Anglo immigrants from the East Coast and the Midwest brought with them the ideal of a formal classroom education. For these families, the establishment of a school was second in importance only to the establishment of the homestead itself. But some immigrants from the European continent feared that formal schooling would hasten their children's loss of the language and culture of the homeland. Furthermore, a significant number of parents felt that school attendance interfered with the necessary work of the child on the homestead.[1] And most Indian parents rightly viewed the establishment of reservation and mission schools as the beginning of the end of their way of life.

The Wisdom of Elders

Traditionally, the education of the Native American child was an informal if integral part of everyday tribal life. According to Indian wisdom, what a child learned during the first twelve years of life was crucial, yet most tribes gave their children considerable latitude in acquiring knowledge and encouraged them to learn and grow at their own pace.[2]

Much of what children learned about the manners and mores of their people was conveyed through stories told by elders—creation myths and trickster stories, leg-

Opposite: While this South Dakota schoolroom boasted all the fine features of turn-of-the-century rural education—an efficient heating system, blackboard, organ, presidential portraits, and the American flag—not every frontier classroom was so finely appointed.

Left: A Kootenai child of western Montana poses with tribal elders, 1895. Within native cultures, education was largely based on an informal tutorial system in which adults of the tribe—particularly the elders—were integrally engaged in a child's training.

115

Above: *Schoolgirls of Hadleyville, Oregon, 1912, share a secret over lunch.*

skills, tribal art forms, and tribal ritual. Among some of the Plains peoples boys and girls were separated at an early age and schooled in different behaviors—including separate male and female patterns of speech and ways of sitting on the ground. In other tribes there was little gender specialization in education until preadolescence. But in all native cultures, from earliest childhood, little girls observed and modeled the work of the women of their tribes, while little boys imitated the ways of the men.[4]

Gradually, imitative play became the real thing. Under the watchful eye of female elders, Navajo girls were taught to weave and Apache girls were taught to make baskets. Young Hidatsa Sioux were taught to plant corn with a pointed stick and to hoe the ground with the shoulder blade of a buffalo. Almost every tribe schooled their young women in food gathering and the identification of plants, in fire making and cooking, and in the art of making soft leather clothing from animal skins. Because women had to guard the camp when men were away, young girls were also taught to take care of horses and to use bows and knives—and later, rifles—to hunt small game.[5]

Boys honed riding and shooting skills under the watchful eyes of their fathers and uncles. They memorized hunting prayers and songs and learned to fast and to wait for favorable signs before going out on a hunt or into battle. They learned to approach their quarry from downwind, to call up a doe by imitating the bleat of a fawn. They were trained in the rules of war and raiding: "Cross open spaces only in darkness," they were told, and "Do not seek the shade on hot days, but lie in tall grass."[6]

Ohiyesa, known later in life as Charles Eastman, learned the things vital to the Sioux way of life under the tutelage of an uncle. "Look closely to everything you see," his uncle would say as the boy left the tipi in the morning. Then each evening, upon the boy's return, the uncle would

ends of the daring exploits of tribal heroes, and tales of memorable battles and hunts. "We knew that these stories were told to teach us how to behave and what to expect," said Delfina Cuero, about her upbringing as a Kumeyaay at the turn of the century in southern California. Through such stories Native American children across the West learned the value of bravery, fortitude, generosity, and wisdom.[3]

Indian children also learned through example, training, and persistent instruction. The Yakama people of what is today the state of Washington assigned expert tutors, many of whom were older relatives, to teach their children practical living

question him closely, sometimes for an hour or more: On which side of the tree is the lighter-colored bark? On which side does the tree have the most regular branches? What birds had he seen? And if Ohiyesa could not describe a bird's color, the shape of its bill, its song, its locality, his uncle would remind him once again to "take a second look at everything you see."[7]

Among the Apache, speed and endurance afoot were as important as horsemanship, and the tribal values of courage and strength were espoused through the regimen of running. Boys were made to run constantly—usually with a pack on their backs. "Be up before daylight and run up the mountain and be back before daylight [tomorrow]," a boy would be told. "Your mind will be developed and your legs will be developed and nobody will be able to outrun you."[8]

While most tribes treated their children with gentle tolerance, the Apache child, like the child of the Crow and the Blackfeet, was exposed to harsh discipline and rigid training. Eating habits of Apache boys were scrutinized, and they grew used to empty bellies. They were expected to dunk themselves in creeks frothed with ice and dry themselves without seeking the comfort of the fire.[9]

Above left: His riding skills already well advanced, an Assiniboine youth sits confidently astride his paint.

Above right: In life—as in this posed portrait—these young Arapaho boys, sons of Sharp Nose, mimicked the adult hunter as they brought down prairie dogs, squirrels, and birds with their youth-sized bows and arrows.

Below: Tension and determination are written on the faces of young Navajo runners lining up for a footrace at the tribe's 1913 Fourth of July celebration. These boys came from a heritage that valued speed and endurance afoot.

Above: In 1890, Frederic Remington's The Indian Method of Breaking a Pony *captured the teamwork of adult and youth in breaking the will of a mustang.*

Right: In the mid-nineteenth century George Catlin sketched Sham Fight by Mandan Boys, *depicting how, at a certain age, free play turned to serious training under the watchful eye of adult warriors.*

Even in less rigid Native American cultures, children sometimes resented the training imparted by their elders. Mourning Dove, a Salish girl who lived in eastern Washington at the turn of the century, remembered the demands placed on her by her mother and grandmother. "I was made to run uphill without stopping until I reached the top of each of the . . .knolls close to our home," she recalled. "[And] I had to carry all the water in the house. If I stopped to pout, I was ordered to run rather than walk to the spring." As an adult, Mourning Dove could see that the running "was intended to strengthen my lungs and increase my wind power. . . . to give me energy for my lifework." But as a young girl she had become resentful when the "pampering" of her early childhood had suddenly stopped. "Deep in my heart," she recalled, "I felt my parents were being most cruel to me."[10]

Reservation and Mission Schools

As the nineteenth century moved to a close, the reservation system as well as the evangelical efforts of various denominations radically altered the education of Native Americans. Federal policy encouraged and supported the establishment of schools that would "civilize and Christianize" tribal children, schools that were a vital part of the government's program to assimilate all Indians into white society. In effect, such schools represented the beginning of the end of tribal customs, patterns, and allegiances.[11]

Little in their traditional educational process had prepared Indian children to function well in an environment in which they were expected to sit in desks in orderly rows and endure the passing of days segmented into precisely timed periods devoted to learning totally unfamiliar subjects like English and mathematics. Even lessons in the physical sciences, lessons that had been learned experientially from earliest childhood within the tribal setting, seemed strange and unfamiliar when presented in textbook form. School also meant the literal loss of one's Indian identity with the forfeiture of one's Indian name and all its associations and the assumption of a new, anglicized name.[12]

Often as not, attending a government or mission school meant leaving home, since many Indian children were sent to boarding schools—some of which were on the reservation but others of which were hundreds of miles distant. Children were sometimes taken away despite the protests of parents and grandparents. Marie Washakie's grandmother objected so strongly to her being taken from home that agency

Above: Boys and girls at Fort Shaw Indian School outside Great Falls, Montana, are shown in the workroom where they were taught handcrafts. This boarding school served students from several different tribes, as well as the children of non-Indian teachers and administrators.

Above: In 1902–1903 the Fort Shaw Indian School fielded a strong girls' basketball team, shown here in their native dress rather than the uniforms they wore on the floor. Most of these young women were still members of the team when it barnstormed its way across the country and defeated all comers at the World's Fair in St. Louis in 1904.

police had to escort the child to the Shoshone Episcopal Girls School. Helen Sekaquaptewa, an eight-year-old Hopi, was also "kidnaped" by agency police and taken to the reservation school against the wishes of parents who opposed an Anglo education for their daughter.[13]

Adjustments to the new way of life were hard. "We had to get used to so many things we had never known before," recalled Luther Standing Bear, a young Teton Sioux who was sent to Carlisle Indian School in Pennsylvania. "Everything was a lot different," according to Pansy St. Clair, a young Shoshone educated in a mission school not far from her home on the Wind River Reservation in Wyoming. "Everything from food, to clothing, to bedding, and going to church—all that was completely different." For Dolly Rowan, another Shoshone child, the greatest difference between home and school was wearing shoes. "[We] didn't know what it was like to wear shoes," she recalled. "Oh, it about killed us off, but we lived through it!"[14]

In 1879, when young Standing Bear set out from the Pine Ridge Reservation in present-day South Dakota, bound for Carlisle, the battle at Little Bighorn, fought some three years earlier, was still fresh in the memories of most white Americans. At rail stops along the route the bewildered Indian children were accosted by crowds of hostile townspeople. "[We were] surrounded by a jeering, unsympathetic people whose only emotions were those of hate and fear," Standing Bear recalled. "[They had] no more understanding of us than if we had suddenly been dropped from the moon."[15]

Once he reached Carlisle, young Standing Bear became Luther, a name arbitrarily chosen from a list written on a blackboard. Then his hair was cut—a sure harbinger of bad luck—and he was fitted for a uniform. The uniform was his sole consolation, countering all the indignities otherwise suffered. "How proud we were with the clothes that had pockets and with boots that squeaked!" he recalled years later.

"We walked the floor nearly all that [first] night. Many of the boys even went to bed with their clothes all on."[16]

But for most children, clothes and new shoes hardly made up for what Peter Iverson has described as "the wrenching departures from home, the separation from family and the homesickness that would not go away." Indeed, one Shosone boy recalled how he hated the uniforms at the Wind River Reservation school—knee pants and black stockings for the younger boys and striped dresses for the girls—and the haircuts, for his short hair and bangs were constant reminders of everything he had had to give up when he was sent away to school.[17]

For the first twelve years of her life, home was a tipi by the Missouri River for Zitkala-sa, or Red Bird—a Yankton Sioux known later as Gertrude Bonnin. Then, in 1889, she and her fifteen-year-old brother were sent away to a Quaker school for Indians in Wabash, Indiana. Unable to understand the language and afraid her braids would be cut off, Zitkala-sa's first instinct after her arrival at the school was to find a place to hide.[18]

Lone Wolf, a Blackfoot, was eight years old in 1893 when he was taken from his parents and sent to Fort Shaw Indian School outside Great Falls, Montana. "It was very cold that day when we were loaded into the wagons," he recalled. "Oh, we cried for this was the first time we were to be separated from our parents. . . . Nobody waved as the wagons, escorted by the soldiers, took us toward the school at Fort Shaw. Once there our belongings were taken from us, even the little medicine bags our mothers had given us to protect us from harm. Everything was placed in a heap and set afire."[19]

Different schools, of course, had different characters—and fostered different memories in their former students. The Shoshone Episcopal Girls School on the Wind River Reservation in Wyoming was recalled fondly in later life by most of the

Above: Educated at St. Xavier's Mission School in eastern Montana, these girls of the Crow tribe posed for their picture on the school steps in 1895. The Anglo child without a uniform, upper center, is probably the daughter of a teacher at the school.

women who had gone there. "First thing you're always kind of scared," one Shoshone woman said of her school experience. "[But] you kind of get used to it [and] I liked the mission [school]. It was just like home. It was a wonderful place for the little Shoshone girls." At any time they felt homesick those little girls could go to a wooden tipi that stood in the middle of the campus, and there they could speak their own language, sing their native songs, and practice traditional arts like beadwork. "I have all good, fond memories of the mission," Vida Haukaas, another Shoshone recalled. "If it weren't for the mission, I don't know what kind of person I would [have wound] up being."[20]

In contrast, the government school on the same reservation seems to have engendered nothing but resentment in most of its alumni. "They'd round the [Indian] kids up and make them go to school whether they wanted to go or not," recalled Dorothy Peche. "They just took [us] down there." Constructed in 1885, the adobe building on the Shoshone Reservation featured barred windows that not only discouraged attacks by hostile tribes but also deterred the escape attempts of unhappy

Right: This pensive Indian youth gives silent testimony to emotional factors that could not always be measured—nor defined—but nevertheless worked to undermine the health of Native American children attending reservation boarding schools.

Death as a Line Item

Some government schools were poorly staffed and poorly supervised. Some suffered from limited funding. Sewage and water systems were not always adequate, and the damp, drafty, overcrowded buildings bred consumption. Between 1899 and 1905, 2 percent of the students at the government school on the Round Valley, California, reservation died each year. Round Valley was hardly unique in this aspect, for the monthly report forms school administrators filed with officials in Washington provided a blank for listing the number of student deaths in that particular month.[a]

The Reverend John Roberts, founder of the Shoshone Episcopal Girls School, wrote to the Bureau of Indian Affairs in 1901 concerning the ill health of his students. "The heavy death rate of the pupils is undoubtedly due to the effect of civilization upon them," he concluded. "In school they have good care, wholesome food, well cooked. They have plenty of fresh air, outdoor exercise and play. Yet under these conditions, in school, they droop and die, while their brothers and sisters, in camp, live and thrive."[b]

---

[a] Wendy Wall, "Gender and the Citizen Indian," in Jameson and Armitage, *Writing the Range*, 210.

[b] From *Trout Creek to Gravy High*.

students. According to Peche, one classmate was so miserable that she continued to seek her freedom—despite the harsh measures used to keep her in school. First one and then two fence posts were shackled to her legs to thwart her attempts at escape. "One [fence post] on each leg," Peche remembered. "And [still] she used to jump out of the window with those two posts . . . she got to where she didn't care."[21]

There were, of course, children who adjusted fairly well to the new life. "They said 'it will get better for you,'" Val Norman recalled. "And gradually I got, you know, used to the routine." The routine varied from school to school, but most reservation schools featured instruction in industrial and domestic trades as well as academic subjects, sometimes dedicating half the day to class work and the other half to field or shop work. Students were trained in blacksmithing, shoe and saddle making, and cooking and sewing. Almost all reservation schools were self-sufficient, having their own gardens, cattle, and chickens. Farm and garden products supplied the school kitchens with foods—spinach and oatmeal, for instance—that were as strange to the boarders as were the other aspects of "civilization" that had become a part of their daily lives.[22]

Attending a mission or reservation school—particularly a boarding school—had profound and lasting effects on Indian children. When Zitkala-sa returned to her reservation in South Dakota three years after having left to go to the Quaker school in Indiana, she found that she could hardly converse with her own mother, so great were the disparities between the Indian culture at home and the white culture she had been exposed to during her schooling. Determined to lessen that disparity, Zitkala-sa—as Gertrude Bonnin—worked effectively to reform Indian policy. Dartmouth-educated Ohiyesa, who became a well-known physician under his Anglo name, Charles Eastman, made his mark in the world beyond the reservation, but the rights of his people remained at the heart of all his work.[23]

While pleased with the visible "success" of pupils like Bonnin and Eastman, government and mission school educators often complained that many of their most promising students returned to the reservation and went "back to the blanket." Helen Sekaquaptewa, a Hopi, and Luther Standing Bear, a Teton Sioux, both returned to their reservations after finishing their schooling, but neither could be said to have gone "back to the blanket," since both worked to bridge the vast cultural gap between reservation life and the outside world.[24]

Settlers' Schools

Settlers' children who had begun their schooling in the East or Midwest generally found the frontier school to be quite different from the classrooms in which they had studied "back home." A settlement's first school was usually a one-room building made of logs or sod and furnished with hard wooden benches, a cast-iron stove, and a large bell that summoned the pupils to class. For drinking water, there was a bucket and dipper; for recreation, an open field; for rest rooms, an outhouse.[25]

The one-room school Ben Walsh attended around the turn of the century in Stutsman County, North Dakota, had three windows on a side, an outdoor privy, and a variable water supply—children from the nearest house were responsible for carrying buckets of water to school each day. The distribution of water varied from school to school and teacher to teacher. "When the water came," Matilda Peitzke Paul recalled of her days in an Iowa schoolhouse, "our teacher would let us pass it, first to teacher then to pupils, all drinking out of the same long-handled tin dipper."[26]

That Iowa schoolhouse was a log cabin where "seats . . . were long benches placed on three sides of the room." There were no desks or tables, though a slanting shelf attached on one wall provided a writing sur-

Above: A dugout with windows to allow ventilation and light served as school-house for this group of Kansas children, ca. 1900.

Below: These southern California scholars, ca. 1890, learned their lessons in a brush-arbor classroom. Only in the arid Southwest could one expect to find a school without walls—and this one offered students the benefits of books and a blackboard, pedagogical tools not always found in frontier schools housed in buildings.

face. "We turned and faced the wall while writing or working arithmetic," Paul remembered.[27]

Such a schoolroom was luxurious compared with the converted chickenhouse in Philbrook, Montana, where Winifred Shipman, a young teacher newly arrived from Vermont, called her first class to order in 1883. There were no desks and, for the first six weeks, no books. Undaunted, Shipman wrote out stories on brown paper for reading lessons, drew maps on the floor for geography lessons, and for science lessons took the children outdoors to study rocks and dissect hawks and rabbits. By the time the coveted books arrived, she had completed the whitewashing of the walls and proudly invited parents and neighbors into the newly furbished building for a Christmas program.[28]

The earliest schools were usually "subscription schools" organized by parents who drew up a program, hired a teacher, and charged families an agreed-upon

amount of tuition for each child. The system of "public education" came only belatedly to frontier communities and states. In the mid-1850s, some three years after the Gay family of Missouri had settled in Lane County, Oregon, neighbors interested in organizing a school "all assembled to talk the matter over." A log structure was eventually built on a site Martin Gay had donated for this purpose, and a committee extended a five-month teaching contract to a man considered "suitable" for the job.[29]

"How glad we were [as we] tripped off that mile to the first day of school," Martha Gay Masterson recalled years later. Martha's three-year-old sister, who had been born on the family's journey across the plains, "was quite young for school but she wanted to go." She was allowed to join her seven siblings on the hike to school, being carried by her big brothers "when she tired."[30]

Students came to school on foot, on horseback, and in wagons, carrying their slates and tablets and dinner pails. Little Ursula Camastral of the Judith Basin in Montana rode five miles on horseback each day to attend school with eight other scholars, some of whom had ridden even farther than she. In good weather Camastral would stake her horse outside the schoolhouse, but in bad weather she left the mare at a nearby ranch and walked the final quarter mile.[31]

Because of the severity of the winters, school terms in Montana and the plains states usually ended in December, with classes reconvening in late spring. Though the school that Matilda Peitzke Paul attended remained in session throughout the winter term, classes were held in the small back room of a neighbor's log home, since the little frame school building could not protect its occupants from the fierce winds and blowing snow of the Iowa prairie. Frontier teachers and parents had a tacit understanding that students would attend school only when the weather permitted.

Because Margaret Archer Murray, another child of 1860s Iowa, "couldent wade deep snow in winter time," she attended school only during the summer session until she was eleven years old, by which time her legs had grown long enough to carry her through the deep drifts.[32]

Frontier Teachers

Teachers were among the most transient members of western communities. Stephanie Prepiora, who spent her girlhood on a farm outside Minto, North Dakota, attended a one-room, one-teacher, all-grades school, where teachers changed yearly. Some were good, Prepiora remembered, some were not, and quite a few had discipline problems with older boys whose education had been frequently interrupted by the farming cycle.[33]

The lives of students in Tualatin, Oregon, were greatly enriched by their interaction with Mary Almira Gray, of Vermont, one of six hundred or so teachers sent west by the National Popular Education Board between 1847 and 1858. Generally well educated and experienced, these young women

---

A Schooner Schoolhouse

The five children of Eliza and Charles Clark learned their lessons under their mother's tutelage in the converted cabin of a shipwrecked schooner that had been dragged from the depths of the Pacific Ocean not far from the Clarks' coastal California home. When the *Anna Lyle* went down in 1876 in a fierce storm off Point Sal, Eliza Clark offered the ship's owner her gold watch in exchange for whatever could be salvaged of the wreck. When divers found the vessel's cabin nearly intact, she had it dragged ashore, where she converted it into a commodious classroom for her offspring.[a]

---

[a] Ethel-May Dorsey, ed., *This Is Our Valley*, 3d ed. (Santa Maria [Calif.] Historical Society, Santa Maria Printers, 1977), 105.

Above: *Almost every child rode to this country school in Jackson County, Colorado, on horseback, ca. 1887. Note that both girls in the picture posed side-saddle for the photograph. Only rarely could a girlchild of this era convince her parents to let her ride astride in public.*

signed a contract that required at least two years of service in the West. Afterward they were free to remain where they were or to return to their homes in the East.[34]

In the absence of such well-qualified teachers, most school boards tended to hire whoever was available and willing to teach. Organizers of Denver's first school recruited Oliver Goldrick after he entered town in a Prince Albert coat cursing his team in Greek, Latin, and Sanskrit. Obviously, teachers recruited in such fashion did not always bring dedication and skills to the job, and many of those who claimed to be prepared to teach had received no pedagogical training and had little experience in presiding over a classroom.[35]

Some teachers were so close in age to their students that setting teacher-student boundaries posed problems. This situation was often exacerbated by the fact that, in the absence of teacherages, most frontier teachers boarded out with one or more families over the course of a school term.

Teachers could become the central person in a frontier child's life. Ann Skocilich Pentilla, who grew up in Butte as the daughter of Croatian immigrants, never forgot her first teacher, Stella McGovern. "Seemed like she just stood out in my mind from the first grade up," Pentilla recalled years later. The beloved teacher was remembered especially for her patience with the little Croatian child who "couldn't talk the American language" when she began school. "A lot of the children couldn't [speak English]," Pentilla remembered, "everybody talked their own language."[36]

Mollie Sheehan's education in Virginia City, Montana Territory, took place over "brief and uncertain periods" of time, and her most memorable teacher was Thomas Dimsdale, a gentle Englishman who commanded a "harmonious and pleasant" classroom. "While his few pupils buzzed and whispered over their variously assorted readers, arithmetics, and copy books," Mollie Sheehan Ronan later recalled, "the professor sat at a makeshift desk near the little window of the log schoolhouse writing, writing, writing, writing" the articles and editorials he was publishing in his newspaper, the *Montana Post*.[37]

Not all teachers were remembered so

Left: *Pictured in 1884 with their youthful teacher in front of the first school "building" erected in Long Beach, California, these young scholars would soon be housed in a more substantial building as the agricultural boom in southern California led to the rapid expansion of the fledgling school system.*

Left: *School-aged children of families posted to Fort Totten, Dakota Territory, in 1881 pose with their classmates—children of civilians living near and/or working at the fort—on the front steps of the fort's administration building.*

*Right: Miss
Stewart, who was
teaching sixth grad-
ers in Bozeman,
Montana, in 1898,
presented personal-
ized holiday greet-
ings to her
students.*

Masterson recalled, "and if he discovered any fun or idleness going on, down would come that switch causing the juveniles to draw themselves into small parcels to evade the rod. How we disliked him!"[38]

Mixed Memories

Despite Ann Skocilich Pentilla's love for her teacher, the little child's difficulty with the English language resulted in failing grades. And in the Butte school system, Pentilla noted, "If you didn't have passing grades, you'd have to make them up [in summer school]. . . . There'd be about nine or ten of us each year and we'd just kind of look forward to it."[39]

For many children, school—even summer school—provided a welcome respite from the work-a-day world. "Most of the year meant drudgery on the farms, and school was a relief from hard work," Mary Lacy Crowder wrote of her childhood in Palo Alto County, Iowa. The children of North Dakota immigrants were generally not allowed to attend school until after the fall harvest, when they could once again be spared by their families. Even in winter, permission to attend school was granted only on the condition that children would carry out their assigned farm chores—both before and after school. As Elizabeth Hampsten's

fondly. Martha Gay Masterson's earliest schooldays were spent in Greene County, Missouri, under a teacher who wore "a long swallowtail coat, said coat being very black and slick." This "cross, surly-looking" man carried "a rod of correction in his hand,"

*Right: This Powell,
Wyoming, "school bus"
was reminiscent of the
wagons that brought the
parents or grandparents of
many of these students
west.*

TEXT BOOKS USED.

Appleton's .... Reader.
" .... Writing.
Pattersons .... Speller.
Selections from different Text-books .... Drawing.
Robinson's .... Arithmetic.
Barnes Language lesson ... Grammar.
Appleton's .... Geography.
Three different kinds ... U.S. History
The Human body) Physiology and Hygiene.
the house I live in)
.... Civil Government.

Received and filed Dec 27 1890
W. F. Grange
Co. Sup't

River .... School Township,
County of Ransom .... Dakota.
To Mr W. F. Grange
Lisbon. N. D
Co, Sup't

SIR:—In compliance with Sec. 86 of the
School law, I submit herewith my report
of the School in sub-district No. 4
of Maple River .... School
Township for the term:
Beginning Sept 15 1890
And Ending Dec 9th 1890
Respectfully,
Madge McLaughlin
Teacher.

Total number of days taught.... 60
Whole number of pupils enrolled.. 21
Average daily attendance.... 18 2/10
Per cent of attendance.... 81 4
Number of visits of County Superintendent.... 0

Number of visits of Sub-Director.... 3
Whole number of books in library including dic-
tionary .... One
Salary of teacher per month.......... $ 37.50
Number of months taught.... Three

DIRECTIONS TO TEACHERS.

1   Give summaries and totals on the other side; the average age, the total number of males and females, the total number of days attended by all, the total absences and the total number in each branch of study.

2.   To find "average age" add the ages of all the pupils and divide the sum by the number of pupils.

3.   "Total number of days taught," means the number of days in the term.

4.   "Whole number of pupils enrolled" should include all pupils attending, whether for a week or the entire term.

5.   "Average daily attendance" should be found by dividing the entire number of days attended by all pupils by the number of days in the term.

6.   "Per cent of attendance" should be found by dividing the entire number of days actually attended by all pupils by the number of days attended by all plus the number of days all were absent, carrying the quotient to two decimal places.

7.   Teachers should be particular and exact in making out these reports as upon them all educational statistics are based for Dakota. Do not omit an item.

8.   Time before the pupil joins and after he withdraws from the school permanently should not be reported as absence.

Give information concerning school and property.

1.   Condition of the school house as to windows, plastering, etc. Does it need any repairs?

Windows are in need of repair.

2.   Condition of furniture   Furniture is in a very good condition

3.   Condition, name, and number of charts, maps, globes, etc. Maps & etc are in good condition. There are three maps. viz–Map Europe. United States & Canada and Map of the World. One globe

4.   Condition of the outhouses as to cleanliness, state of repair, etc. Clean but in need of repair

5.   Have you inspected the outhouses regularly? I have

Above and left: *At the end of December 1890, Madge McLaughlin, a teacher in rural Ransom County, North Dakota, filed this report concerning conditions in her school, listing the texts she had used and citing the need for repair of the windows and the outhouse.*

work with reminiscences of North Dakota pioneers led her to conclude, "Education was not valued; . . . work was what was important, and education [was] merely a distraction from work."[40]

School was a distraction most young scholars welcomed. Matilda Peitzke Paul attended an "ungraded" school in Iowa where she "started at the front of [the] book at the beginning of every term and went as far as [she] could, then start[ed] all over again at the beginning of [the] next term." Despite the apparent monotony in such an educational process, Paul declared, "It still thrills me when I think of [my schooling]."[41]

Minnie Rietz, who grew up on a ranch outside Rock Creek, Wyoming, remembered her school days as fondly as did Paul. Her 1880s classroom had "good desks, maps and a globe, good blackboards," and her teachers were all "well-educated, capable women," who began each school day with "opening exercises" consisting of "a

Above: *Located in the foothills of the Absaroka Mountains, Pine Creek School south of Livingston, Montana, boasted a playground that was big as all the outdoors. On a spring day in 1898, the teacher directs her students in a game of ring-around-the-rosy.*

chapter from the Bible and fifteen minutes of calisthenics." Rietz studied from "Mc-Guffy's Readers, Mentieth's Geography, Davies' Arithmetic, Reed and Kellogg's Grammar, Barnes' History and Physiology, Spencerian Copy Books, White's Speller and English Composition," books bought by her parents and carefully "covered with an oilcloth wrapper . . . to keep the covers clean."[42]

In her 1860 classroom in Homer, Iowa, twelve-year-old Becky Williams studied "Geography. Small Arithmetic. Reading. Writeing. And Spelling." Her sister, Bella, a year older, studied those same subjects, although "Phylosophy" and "Grammer" were substituted for "small Arithmetic."[43]

Playground games for rural frontier children included such old favorites as tag, crack-the-whip, and run sheep run during warm-weather sessions. In the winter, recess found children making snow forts and snow figures or sliding down snow-covered hills or across frozen ponds. When the weather was too cold for students to be outside, Minnie Rietz and her classmates played such indoor games as "drop the handkerchief, London Bridge, farmer in the dell."[44]

Mollie Sheehan and her best friend and classmate, Carrie Crane, took recess at their own volition. Whenever Professor Dimsdale seemed especially engrossed with his "writing, writing, writing," Mollie and Carrie would "ask to be excused," then run down to a corral at the bottom of Virginia City's Daylight Gulch and "spend a few thrillful moments sliding down the straw stacks."[45]

Secondary Education

Despite the varying competence of their teachers, the sporadic nature of their sessions, and the relative simplicity of their curricula, rural schools still managed to inspire in many students a desire for secondary education. Some sought further schooling because they realized a good education was the key to a better life. "We were looking forward to the time when we could leave the farm and do something else, preferably in a town or city," Iowa farmgirl Mary Lacy Crowder remembered, "so there was a good deal of speculation

A Study in Contrasts

In 1876, at the age of fifteen, Mary Hunter of Hunter's Hot Springs, a rudimentary spa in Montana Territory, was sent to St. Vincent's Academy in Helena by her parents, who wanted her to have the best available cultural and educational opportunities.

Staffed by the Sisters of Charity, St. Vincent's attracted girls from all over the territory, "irrespective of religion." Indeed, reflecting in later years, Mary Hunter Doane, who was Protestant, estimated that probably "not more than ten" of the fifty boarders were Catholic. Nor was religion emphasized as an academic subject, though music, penmanship, needlework, and "general studies" were. The school term ran from September to June, and classes were held from nine to twelve and from one to four, five days a week.

Expressing both admiration and affection for the nuns who taught her, Doane described them as "young [and] broad in their interests and abilities." She recalled that "the girls often romped with them sometimes to the point of roughness, sometimes seizing caps, and pulling cap strings." On their customary Sunday afternoon hike, the girls were accompanied by at least two of the nuns, who despite their natural exuberance, always kept their charges under "careful" supervision.

That supervision extended to watchful concern for the health of each student. "As soon as a girl felt unwell she was separated from the others," Doane recalled, and if she did not respond quickly to "home treatment," the doctor was called in. Not surprisingly, this enthusiastic boarder experienced not a single day of homesickness during her tenure at St. Vincent's.[a]

The experiences of George Stearns of Roseburg, Oregon, who was also fifteen years old when he was sent away to boarding school, stand in sharp contrast to those of Mary Doane. Although at first George wrote home of satisfying progress in his studies and assured his mother that he was "happy and contented" at Bishop Scott Academy, an Episcopal school in Portland, his attitude underwent an abrupt change soon after he learned that he would not be able to visit his family over the Christmas holidays. His letters thereafter reveal his overwhelming homesickness. There were only ten boarders and thirteen day students enrolled at Bishop Scott for that 1862–63 term, and George grew increasingly lonely for his four younger brothers. Before the spring term officially ended, Almira Stearns gave in to her son's entreaties, and George was soon home in Roseburg, having, in his mother's opinion, "grown a good deal and . . . improved in his appearance" during his months at Bishop Scott Academy.[b]

---

[a] Mary Hunter Doane, Reminiscences, SC 638, Montana Historical Society, Helena.

[b] Peavy and Smith, *Women in Waiting*, 108, 110–14.

Above, left: *By early 1900, Montana schoolboy Horace Thompson, Jr., was attending a military academy away from home.*

Above, right: *The members of this Cheyenne, Wyoming, physical education class studied calisthenics under Professor Stark in 1884.*

the first day of school as to how much help the teacher was likely to be as a stepping-stone to our ambition."[46]

Long after most town children had access to secondary schooling, obtaining a high school education posed special problems for rural students. Some traveled long distances on a daily basis. Once Marie and Ella Papke had completed eighth grade in a Bridger Canyon school, they rode eight miles into Bozeman, Montana, on horseback every morning in order to attend classes at Gallatin County High. Other rural youngsters boarded with townspeople during the school week. Martha Gay of rural Lane County, Oregon, lived with a family in Eugene from Monday through Friday during the winter months, going home each weekend.[47]

Boarding schools were another option for rural students seeking a high school education, though not many homesteading families could afford the fees charged by such institutions. When St. Paul's School for Girls opened in 1872 in Walla Walla, Washington Territory, with three boarders and twenty day scholars, a set of gold scales

was kept in the school office to weigh the dust with which some parents paid tuition. For one of the three boarders, payment was made in the form of beef on the hoof, and potatoes paid the fees of the second boarder. The third arrived for her first term at school astride one of the animals in a mule team returning from carrying provisions into British Columbia.[48]

In the Hispanic Southwest, the male children of the privileged class enjoyed the best of education, either at home under the instruction of private tutors or at elite boarding schools in the East, in Mexico—or even in Madrid. In the 1830s, Juan José de la Guerra of Santa Barbara, California, was educated at a Jesuit school in England, while his younger brothers were sent to school in Mexico City. The scion of a Californio family, Juan José wrote home of his studies in Latin, ancient history, geography, chemistry, and the natural sciences. In contrast to the schooling enjoyed by their brothers, the daughters of this same family received a rudimentary education commensurate with their future roles as wives and mothers.[49]

Deprivation and Discrimination

For some parents, getting a child admitted into school at all was problematic. A law passed in 1847 excluded blacks from Iowa's public schools, and in 1859 California closed its public schools to nonwhites, barring "children of inferior races"—Chinese, Indians, and blacks—from sitting in the same classrooms with white children. With no public schooling available, Chinese parents hired tutors or saw to the education of their offspring themselves. By 1884 the Chinese Consolidated Benevolent Association had opened a school for Chinese children in San Francisco.[50]

"There is scarcely a village or town in California that possesses a common school for the education of Colored children," a black journalist editorialized in 1857—yet black parents were obliged to pay taxes for the support of the schools from which their children were excluded. The situation was untenable, the journalist concluded, since "without schools for the education of those who are to compose the next generation of actors on this great stage, we cannot expect our condition to be permanently improved."[51]

In 1860, in accordance with her maternal grandfather's dying wish, the teen-aged Thoc-me-tony (known later in life as Sarah Winnemucca) was sent to the Academy of Notre Dame de Namur, a convent school in San Jose, California. But the wealthy parents of her white classmates objected to the presence of an Indian child, and after only three weeks, the nuns were forced to send her home to her people in western Nevada.[52]

The sons and daughters of poor families in the Southwest received little formal education beyond that provided in mission outposts by the Franciscan friars or, in the larger towns, by religious orders like the Sisters of Charity of Cincinnati, who established both day and boarding schools for the disadvantaged in Santa Fe, New Mexico, and in Trinidad, Colorado. At San Gabriel Mission in southern Califor-

nia, little girls of seven, eight, and nine years were brought to the mother superior, an Indian nun, to be cared for and taught there until they left the mission to marry.[53]

Clearly, educational opportunities in the trans-Mississippi West varied widely. According to historian Richard White, western states generally did well in providing for the schooling of urban white children and poorly in providing educational opportunities for nonwhite children and rural children. But the situation varied from state to state. California's willingness to levy taxes for the support of its schools produced what was reputed to be the best nineteenth-century educational system in the nation—albeit a discriminatory one. Yet as late as 1870 Nevada still had only thirty-eight schools, or about seven for

Above: Barred from attending California's public schools, this young Chinese boy was tutored in the language and culture of his homeland by a private teacher.

Above: *Although several western states, notably Iowa and California, did not allow "children of inferior races" in public classrooms, in Colorado black children were educated alongside their white classmates, as shown in this 1890s Central City school picture.*

Right: *A young boy and his teacher at the piano at the California School for the Deaf in Berkeley, California, in the early part of the twentieth century.*

Left: The children—and young adults—who attended this one-room schoolhouse in Kenneth, Idaho Territory, could likely attest to the less-than-ideal learning conditions cited in official reports filed with territorial governments. Because of the rough board construction and tiny window, the school could hardly have provided sufficient heat and light for the scholars, though ventilation was not likely a problem.

every one thousand school-aged children.[54]

In 1873 one official found most schoolhouses in Montana Territory "a terror to behold." At about that same time an Oregon school examiner's biennial report noted that little care was taken of the "wretched and ill-located" school buildings after they were built. "Some of our school houses are so delapidated . . . that they are hardly fit for decent people to enter," the official reported. "And yet these are the places to which we send our boys and girls to have them trained up to become intelligent men and women."[55]

Whatever the merits or faults of that "training up," the achievement of educational goals was only one of many rites of passage undergone by children in the trans-Mississippi West.

Passages

Coming of Age on the Frontier

For the most part, childhood ended earlier for youngsters on the frontier than for those in the East. Because responsibilities were assumed at such an early age, adolescence was already giving way to adulthood by the time a child was barely into the teen years. Among Native American tribes spiritual quests and other rituals served as guideposts for a youth's passage into adulthood. Settlers' children made this transition largely without ceremony, aside from bar mitzvahs and confirmations, religious rites that had relatively little impact on a young person's status or treatment in the secular world.

Indian Youth in Transition

For Native Americans childhood typically ended soon after the age of ten, and transition into adulthood was often signaled by the accomplishment of some significant feat. Among the Nootka of the Pacific Northwest a boy's first kill and a girl's first clams were the occasion for feasting and celebration. Among the Tsimshian, another coastal tribe, boys and girls went through a change-of-name ceremony at puberty. Among the Tewa of the Southwest the end of the carefree, innocent days of early childhood was marked by a four-day ritual, after which the Tewa youth was given new status in the tribe.[1]

In almost all tribes patterns of play began to change around the time of puberty, and boys and girls were no longer allowed to play together. A boy would enter into rough sports with comrades his own age, and a girl would begin to spend the larger part of her day working with the women of her family. Putting behind them the occupations of childhood, they began serious preparation for adulthood.[2]

Coming-of-age practices associated with almost all tribes were designed to help youngsters, both male and female, to attain spiritual power. Certain spirits were sought out in specific locations—on mountaintops or buttes or in caves, pools, or waterfalls. Through fasts and rituals the questers sought to connect with these spirits. What they experienced during these rites had a deep and lasting influence on their lives, for in order to be a productive adult, each Indian boy and girl needed the guardianship of a wakan, a powerful spirit guide.[3]

Sioux girls, like girls from many other tribes, underwent a ritual whereby they sought their spirits, but that ritual was gen-

Opposite: Boys on the verge of manhood pose in the aisle of a Wyoming store, ca. 1900.

Below: According to George Catlin, chronicler of native life in mid-nineteenth-century America, "A young man . . . [of an] age to take his place among the ranks of warriors requires a shield, which he makes of the skin of the buffalo's neck." As the shield hardens over a slow fire, members of the tribe dance around it, chanting sacred songs.

Above: A menstrual hut such as this was used by Salish girls of the Pacific Northwest to purify themselves during their first menses and to contemplate womanly ways during the days of their isolation.

time a Tlingit girl experiencing her first menses was kept in a dark hut varied according to the status of her family. Southern Paiute girls were forbidden to eat meat or salt or to drink cold water during their first menses. A Shoshone girl lived in isolation during her first period, and shortly thereafter her parents arranged her marriage.[5]

At the time of a Cheyenne girl's first menses her father would call out to the camp that his daughter had become a woman, and if he was well-to-do, he might give away a horse to mark the occasion. An older woman helped the girl unbraid her hair and bathe herself. Then her body was painted red and she was seated near a fire. Sprinkling a red-hot coal with sweet grass, juniper needles, and white sage, the girl bent over the fire so that the smoke engulfed her body. She then went into the menstrual lodge, where her grandmother cared for her and gave her instructions in the ways of obedience, kindness, gentility, and dutifulness. When her period was over, the girl would again purify herself by passing through the smoke before returning to her home.[6]

To honor her first menstruation, a Navajo girl rose at dawn on the initial day of her period and began a four-day ritual known as Kinaalda. As the sky lightened, the girl would run toward the east for perhaps half a mile. Turning back, she would run to her starting point, only to sprint to the east again, all the while singing, "The breeze coming from her as she runs is beautiful." Each lap was longer than the last, for how far the girl ran determined how long she would live. The running ritual was intended to build courage, mold character, and increase fertility. A girl who shortened her course, or stopped to rest, betrayed a lazy spirit and invited misfortune.[7]

Though the particulars of passage for a young male might vary from tribe to tribe, the process often included sweat baths and periods of isolation and fasting in the woods and mountains. When a Sioux boy

erally associated with the onset of the first menses. In a dense thicket or grove some distance from the village, the menstrual hut, a small tipi, was erected. There the girl was left in isolation or was cared for by her mother or an elder and given instruction in "womanly ways." "Nobody just talked about these things," recalled Delfina Cuero, a Kumeyaay from southern California. "It was all in the songs and myths . . . . All that a girl needed to know to be a good wife, and how to have babies and to take care of them was learned at the ceremony at the time when a girl became a woman."[4]

In the Pacific Northwest, the length of

reached the age of twelve, he entered a sweat lodge, a small hut, where he poured water over heated stones. Then, as the hut filled with steam, he offered certain prayers. When that ritual was completed, he was taken far from the village and left alone for four days and nights without food or water. He was then led back to the village and brought into the presence of the medicine man, to whom he confided what he had seen and heard during his fast. This vision was then celebrated at a feast, and the boy thereafter took his place among the men of the tribe.[8]

Among some Plains tribes a boy's passage might come after he had killed his first buffalo—usually a calf brought down when the boy was in his early teens. His father would cry out the news to the whole camp, and if he could afford it, he would announce the gift of a good horse to a deserving person. At about the same time the boy might go out with his father or an uncle on a war

Left: Daughters of the Cheyenne chief American Horse in early adolescence at the turn of the twentieth century. The elder girl holds evergreen branches used in the ceremonial rites that marked a girl's passage into womanhood.

Below: The younger sisters of these Hopi maidens are already anticipating the day when they will be old enough to adopt the dress and hair style of a young woman who has come of age.

Right: *These courting couples were sketched by Wo Haw, a Kiowa artist, ca. 1870. In most tribes, a young man in mid-teens who had proved his courage through various tests of strength and endurance could begin to court the female of his fancy.*

party, another event that moved him toward manhood.[9]

In his early teens, the Lakota youth Jumping Badger still bore the nickname "Slow" for his deliberate manner—despite his known speed of foot and notable success as a hunter. In his fourteenth year Slow was pronounced good enough and skilled enough to be taken along on his first war party. In the company of ten Lakota warriors he set out on a strike against the Crow. During the skirmish that followed, he counted his first coup, knocking a Crow from his horse. The act elevated Slow to the rank of warrior. His childhood was over. At the ensuing feast, his father placed a white eagle feather upright in his hair, presented him with his own string of horses, painted him black from head to foot to symbolize victory, and gave him the buffalo-hide shield of the warrior. Then, as the ultimate gift, Sitting Bull bestowed his own name on his son. Henceforth the young warrior would be known as Sitting Bull and his father, the chief, as Jumping Bull.[10]

In their midteens, as young men became more and more established within the male society of their clans, they began to court the women of their fancy, though they rarely married until they owned a string of horses, a sign of their virility and relative wealth.[11]

Settlers' Daughters

For settlers' children, especially settlers' daughters, the passage into adolescence tended to be a far less structured affair than it was for native children. In contrast to the celebratory spirit with which an Indian girl welcomed her first menses, non-Indian women often experienced fear or shame at the onset of their first period. One Montana homesteader recalled her horror at finding blood on the back of the dappled-gray horse she had just ridden home from school. When she ran into the barn to ask her father to look after her "injured" horse, he sent her to her mother. "She told me to go and wash between my legs," the woman recalled. "And she showed me how to fold the cloth and snug it into place. I could not believe all that blood had come from me."[12]

There was often a rather dramatic shift from girlhood to womanhood without the luxury of a period of adolescence in which adult responsibilities could be shouldered gradually. Magdalena Martin, daughter of

Left: A 1913 Lutheran confirmation class in eastern Montana. For young Anglo- and Euro-Americans, a religious ritual such as confirmation was the culture's closest equivalent to the more elaborate rites of passage observed by youths from Indian cultures.

German-Russian immigrants, was fourteen when the family set up housekeeping in a boxcar in Ashley, North Dakota. Lena shared those cramped quarters with her parents and six siblings as well as her aunt and uncle and their child. Belatedly, her father realized how difficult the situation had been for Lena. "She was in her adolescence, with no privacy whatever," he recalled, "and we did not even recognize a girl's needs. We shrugged off having any kind of conversation to explain to her the stages of human development. . . . The less said and the more children were kept in ignorance, the better."[13]

Even if a girl's coming of age was not formally celebrated or even openly acknowledged by her family, her entry into womanhood did not go unnoticed by the eligible bachelors in the area. With women scarce in mining towns, young girls were often courted when they were barely into their teens. Only twelve years old when she attended her first dance in Virginia City, Montana Territory, Mollie Sheehan was one of the relatively few females in at-

tendance and was therefore sought out by many young men. As candles flickered in sconces stuck into the log walls and a fiddler played away at familiar tunes, Mollie changed partners many times over the course of the evening. At the time the shy girl was uncomfortable with all the attention, but as she moved into her teens, invitations to dance became increasingly welcome.[14]

At the age of fifteen, four years after her arrival in the West, Lucy Henderson, was married. "In those days the young men wondered why a girl was not married if she was still single when she was sixteen," Henderson recalled. Within a year of her emigration from Missouri to Oregon, Mamie Gay, still in her midteens, was married. Her father went to nearby Portland to buy her wedding outfit, and the ceremony held in the parlor of the family's newly finished log house was "short and impressive." According to Mamie's younger sister, Martha, the bride beamed, her father was distraught at the loss of the daughter who had been his "pet from infancy," and the

Right: *Wyoming siblings on the verge of adolescence pose in front of their log cabin in 1899.*

Opposite, above: *The queen and her court were a major attraction at the annual Sweet Pea Festival in Bozeman, Montana, and each girl in the court of 1906 no doubt dreamed of someday assuming the regal role herself.*

Opposite, below: *A wedding group in Santa Fe, 1912. It was customary for Hispanic girls, like the bride in this photo, to marry while still in their teens.*

steady patter of an autumn rain served as the wedding march.[15]

In Mormon communities where polygyny was still practiced, men were always open to adding a younger wife to the family. The new bride generally lived with or near the older wives, from whom she learned much about her responsibilities as a wife and mother.

Many Hispanic girls married in their middle teens and were mothers before they reached their eighteenth birthday. Maria Inocente Pico de Avila, daughter of a wealthy Californio family, was only beginning to read and write when she was taken from school to begin preparation for life as wife and mother. "Many girls never even finished these few studies," she said, "because their mothers nearly always took them from school to marry them off." Maria bore life-long resentment of "the bad custom of marrying girls very young,"

recalling, "I only stayed in school until my fourteenth year. Then my mother took me to the ranch to prepare me to work, and at 15 years and 8 months of age I was married."[16]

Despite compelling cultural imperatives stressing marriage and childbearing as the most acceptable career for young women, some frontier adolescents took jobs that seemed to hold the promise of long-range independence and security. A young woman of Butte, Montana, began working at Lutey Brothers Grocery in 1909 while she was still in her early teens. "It was a wonderful place for a kid to go for the reason that you never heard a swear word," she later recalled. Mr. Lutey looked after his young workers "like a father," hosting parties and sleigh rides for his growing force of employees.[17]

By the time Ollie French reached adolescence, she was living with her mother in the servants' quarters of a home owned by the Frick family of Elbert, Colorado, handling endless cleaning, laundry, sewing, and cooking chores in exchange for room, board, and a modicum of cash—an experience that convinced young Ollie there must be better ways of earning a living.[18] Many young teens worked away from home as "hired girls" or domestics or "mother's helpers," and even the ones who boarded out with the families they served often continued to turn their wages over to their parents, who were struggling to feed and clothe younger children still living at home.

Assuming her schooling was over by the time she finished eighth grade, Ellen Dute, who grew up in Grand Forks County, North Dakota, went to work on her parents' farm, driving the four-horse team that pulled the plow, the drag, the disk, and the harvester and binder. After a few years of work in which she "froze in the spring and late fall, and suffered the heat of summer," she was more than ready to enroll in a one-year course of teacher preparation that qualified her for work in the state's rural schools.[19]

Above: A Minnesota lad
has his hair clipped in readi-
ness for the Saturday night
dance, ca. 1915.

Settlers' Sons

Boys were not nearly so likely to be pushed into early marriage. When fifteen-year-old George Stearns of Roseburg, Oregon, attended a "grand-opening ball" at the American Hotel in 1863, his mother reported that the dance had seemed to "set him crazy." Having enjoyed his social debut, the boy subsequently went to "a kitchen Party," a gathering of young people where dancing was again the featured entertainment. "It seems strange to have him going around," Almira Stearns wrote to her husband, Daniel, who was working in the mines of the Salmon River country, "but I suppose he must have some Amusements and he had better dance than to visit Saloons." Anxious about single-parenting the teenager in Roseburg where "drinking and Gambling are the chief amusements night and day sundays and all," Almira observed, "It seems to me that boys raised in Oregon are of no account." Resolving to keep her eldest son busy with work and school, she soon sent George away to a boarding school in Portland. Before the end of the spring term he had returned home to Roseburg, where he began clerking in a local store. Since his compensation included room and board, George Stearns was effectively on his own the summer before he turned sixteen.[21]

One sign of a young farm boy's coming of age was his hiring out on threshing crews or as a sheepherder, employment that often took him away from home. To earn the money for schooling in the East, young Henry Shipman spent the summer of 1884 living in a sheepherder's wagon some distance from his parents' home in Montana Territory's Judith Basin. As the sons of Montana pioneer David Christie moved into their teen years, they took on more and more responsibility in their father's dairy operation, and each of the boys in turn was given a dairy cow as the basis for building a herd of his own.[22]

Charles Clark of Portland, Oregon, was twelve years old in 1859 when he and his

With teachers in demand in frontier communities, many young women already had classrooms of their own by the time they were fifteen or sixteen. Some of these young school marms viewed teaching as a convenient way to earn a living until they could find a suitable husband and begin their own family, but others, like Erikka Hansen of South Dakota, came to realize that a single woman who taught could aspire to claiming and working her own homestead.[20] The example of Hansen and other women who chose, early on, an independent working life was no doubt important to those adolescent girls who were less than eager for the early marriages so common among their peers.

father left his pregnant mother and little brother behind and set out to work the family's homestead claim near Walla Walla, Washington Territory. Although Charles was the only white boy in the whole valley that spring—except for the officers' sons at Fort Walla Walla—he had the company of his father, with whom he shared a small tent, and of the Indian children who lived around the Clark homestead. And he had plenty of work as well. He and his father labored long and hard to turn over the virgin ground and sow their first crop of oats. They also planted young fruit trees that would soon be their orchard.

But there was a weekly respite from the hard work. On Sundays the father and son would go into town, an excursion Charles always enjoyed, even though Walla Walla of the late 1850s was little more than "a mongrel collection of shacks and tents, with a confused mass of settlers, Indians and soldiers straying through" and its chief amusements were "horse racing and gambling."

That summer, when Ransom Clark returned to Portland for his wife and little Will, he left Charles on the homestead claim to share the tent with Robert Horton, a family friend, and to plow a neighbor's fields in return for the logs the man was providing for the Clarks' new cabin. Several weeks later Charles received word that his father had died of a virulent disease on his way back to the Walla Walla homestead with his wife and little boy. A day after receiving this somber news, Charles met his mother and brother at Walla Walla. Though she had been strongly advised to give up the claim and return to Oregon, his mother listened to Charles's assurances that he could do the work needed to realize his father's dream, and she agreed to hold on.

Once again leaving Charles to see to things, his mother went back to Portland to have her baby. By the time she returned to the homestead that October with little Will and a six-week-old infant, Charles

Young Professionals on Horseback

For many frontier boys, skill with a horse led to early entry into the adult world. George Jackson of the Judith Basin in Montana Territory was only fourteen when he began his career as a cowboy by hiring on with various ranchers during spring and fall roundups. As a fifteen-year-old, George took part in the gruesome spring roundup of the frozen carcasses of the hundreds of cattle that had perished on the open range during the record-setting winter of 1886–87. On the basis of that experience, the young man vowed that he would never own cattle that he could not afford to feed through the winter.[a]

Born into slavery in Tennessee in 1854, Nat Love left the South and his family behind at the age of fifteen and set out for the West. At Dodge City, Kansas, he joined up with a group of cowboys and began the career that made him a part of the legend surrounding the historic cattle drives that brought millions of animals from Texas to Kansas and points north.[b]

The young boys who rode for the Pony Express from April 1860 to October 1861 enjoyed instant fame and recognition. Advertising for "young, skinny, wiry fellows, not over 18. . . . Orphans preferred," the firm of Russell, Majors, and Waddell picked up, in all, some two hundred expert young riders, including fourteen-year-old William Cody, James Butler Hickok, and two young African Americans, William Robinson and George Monroe. Their assignment was to carry the mail between the 190 stations situated across the two thousand miles from St. Joseph, Missouri, to Sacramento, California. The brief but storied operation came to a close when transcontinental telegraph service was initiated in October of 1861. Even with young riders like Buffalo Bill Cody, Wild Bill Hickok, Bill Robinson, and George Monroe, the Pony Express was no match for the Western Union.[c]

[a] Deal and McDonald, *Heritage Book of Original Fergus County Area*, 158.

[b] Katz, *Black West*, 150–51.

[c] Werner, *Pioneer Children*, 152; Katz, *Black West*, 128; *Encyclopedia Americana* (1958), 22: 353.

Above: In a Montana wheat field, a teenaged boy works alongside his father.

Below: By 1890, thirteen-year-old Fred Kessler, the young man on the far right, has already taken his place in his father's brewery in Helena, Montana.

was able to point with pride to the log cabin that he, Robert Horton, and an uncle had nearly completed and to the garden plot that he was preparing for her use in the spring. With the departure of the two older men, young Charles Clark became, by his own report, "the nearest man about the place."[23]

While the coming-of-age experiences of Charles Clark were somewhat similar to those of other frontier children, the specifics of the boy's upbringing and of his overnight passage into adulthood are unique. His gender, his family's economic status, and his father's early death all directly affected his childhood. He was influenced as well, though less directly, by cultural expectations, environmental factors, and political power shifts—the same sorts of variables that affected the lives of all children who came of age in the trans-Mississippi West.

Thus, as historian Elliott West has observed, whatever their particular circumstance, frontier children more or less grew up with the country. And, as many of the visual and verbal images in this pictorial overview would suggest, their lives were profoundly shaped—for better or worse—by that reality.

Above: While farm boys—and sometimes girls—took on heavy fieldwork in their early teens, urban youths moved into various mercantile and professional apprenticeships. Here a young resident of Butte, Montana, takes his place behind the counter of Lutey Brothers Grocery Store, one of the earliest self-service groceries in the turn-of-the-century West.

Notes

An Infinite Variety:
Childhood on the Frontier

1. Ruth Barnes Moynihan, "Children and Young People on the Overland Trail," *Western Historical Quarterly* 6, no. 3 (July 1975): 294.

2. See, among others, Elliott West, *Growing Up with the Country: Childhood on the Far Western Frontier* (Albuquerque: University of New Mexico Press, 1989); Elizabeth Hampsten, *Settlers' Children: Growing Up on the Great Plains* (Norman: University of Oklahoma Press, 1991); Emmy Werner, *Pioneer Children on the Journey West* (San Francisco: Westview Press, 1995); Rebecca Stefoff, *Children of the Westward Trail* (Brookfield, Conn.: Millbrook Press, 1996); N. Ray Hiner and Joseph Hawes, eds., *Growing Up in America: Children in Historical Perspective* (Urbana: University of Illinois Press, 1985); and Elliott West and Paula Petrik, eds., *Small Worlds: Children and Adolescents in America, 1850–1950* (Lawrence: University Press of Kansas, 1992).

3. Marion Gridley, *American Indian Women* (New York: Hawthorn Books, 1974), 4.

4. Marilyn Holt, *The Orphan Trains: Placing Out in America* (Lincoln: University of Nebraska Press, 1992), 4–5; Hiner and Hawes, 83.

5. Holt, 5.

6. Werner, 4.

7. Hampsten, *Settlers' Children*, 13–14.

8. Lorin Brown, with Charles Briggs and Marta Weigle, *Hispano Folklife of New Mexico* (Albuquerque: University of New Mexico Press, 1978), 8; Dorothy Hoobler and Thomas Hoobler, *The Mexican American Family Album* (New York: Oxford University Press, 1994), 27.

9. Nell Irwin Painter, *Exodusters: Black Migration to Kansas after Reconstruction* (Lawrence: University Press of Kansas, 1986), xv.

10. Annette White-Parks, "Beyond the Stereotypes: Chinese Pioneer Women in the American West," in Elizabeth Jameson and Susan Armitage, eds., *Writing the Range: Race, Class, and Culture in the Women's West* (Norman: University of Oklahoma Press, 1997), 261; Milton Meltzer, *The Chinese Americans* (New York: Thomas Crowell, 1980), 81–82.

Ebb and Flow:
Frontier Children on the Move

1. Stefoff, 13.

2. Jennifer Fleischner, *The Apaches* (Brookfield, Conn.: Millbrook Press, 1994), 24.

3. Werner, 2.

4. Moynihan, 292.

5. Martha Gay Masterson, *One Woman's West: Recollections of the Oregon Trail and Settling the Northwest Country 1838–1916*, ed. Lois Barton (Eugene, Ore.: Spencer Butte Press, 1986), 1.

6. Moynihan, 279; Patricia Dean, "Children in Montana," *Montana The Magazine of Western History* 34 (Winter 1984): 38.

7. Stefoff, 33–34.

8. Masterson, 27.

9. Shannon Applegate, *Skookum: An Oregon Pioneer Family's History and Lore* (New York: William Morrow, 1988), 39–41.

10. Bobbie Deal and Loretta McDonald, *The Heritage Book of the Original Fergus County Area* (Lewistown, Mont.: Fergus County Bicentennial Heritage Committee, 1976), 156, 160.

11. Werner, 116.

12. Werner, 19

13. Nancy Wilson Ross, *Westward the Women* (San Francisco: North Point Press, 1985), 7–8.

14. Deal and McDonald, 156.

15. Werner, 115, 152.

16. Moynihan, 284; Frances Milne, "Dust, Stickers, and Mud," *Overland Journal*, Winter 1985: 16–25, 18.

17. Werner, 115; Linda Peavy and Ursula Smith, *The Gold Rush Widows of Little Falls: A Story Drawn from the Letters of Pamelia and James Fergus* (St. Paul: Minnesota Historical Society Press, 1990), 183.

18. Moynihan, 282.

19. Moynihan, 287.

20. Werner, 30.

21. Moynihan, 290.

22. Margaret Ronan, "Memoirs of a Frontier Woman: Mary C. Ronan," master's thesis, State University of Mon-

tana, 1932, 33; Moynihan, 293; Werner, 118.

23. Juanita Brooks, *Emma Lee* (Logan: Utah State University Press, 1984), 56.

24. Moynihan, 283.

25. Masterson, 40–41.

26. Deal and McDonald, 161.

27. Masterson, 37.

28. Moynihan, 282–83; Georgia Willis Read, "Women and Children on the Oregon-California Trail in the Gold-Rush Years," *Missouri Historical Review* 39 (October 1944): 1–23, (quotations, 14–15).

29. Moynihan, 280.

30. Read, 14.

31. Moynihan, 292.

32. Stefoff, 65.

33. Milne, 16.

34. Milne, 19.

35. Read, 12; Linda Peavy and Ursula Smith, *Pioneer Women* (New York: Smithmark, 1996; Norman: University of Oklahoma Press, 1997), 41.

36. Read, 22, 23; Werner, 75.

37. Werner, 21.

38. Stefoff, 73.

39. Masterson, 37, 43–44.

40. Lillian Schlissel, *Women's Diaries of the Westward Journey* (New York: Schocken Books, 1982), 180–81, 185.

41. Moynihan, 282, 286–87.

42. Moynihan, 287.

43. Moynihan, 287.

44. Werner, 30, 24.

45. Moynihan, 293.

46. Read, 23.

47. Read, 11.

48. Milne, 20.

49. Dean, 38.

50. Werner, 20–21.

51. Masterson, 79–82.

52. Linda Peavy and Ursula Smith, *Women in Waiting in the Westward Movement: Life on the Home Frontier* (Norman: University of Oklahoma Press, 1994), 94–95.

53. Edna Smith Head, "Recollections of Peter and Elizabeth Levengood," in Mae Botten's unpublished history, held by Shirley Levengood Bachini of Havre, Montana; Peavy and Smith, *Gold Rush Widows*, 207.

54. Head.

55. Peavy and Smith, *Women in Waiting*, 230.

56. Levy, *They Saw the Elephant* 153; White-Parks, 266.

57. White-Parks, 259.

Homes and Habitats:
Frontier Children and Their Environment

1. Robert Utley, *The Lance and the Shield: The Life and Times of Sitting Bull* (New York: Henry Holt, 1993), 4–6. The Hunkpapa were a band within the larger Lakota group.

2. *Indians of the Plains* (New York: American Heritage, 1960), 34–39.

3. *Cycles of Life* (Alexandria, Va.: Time-Life Books, 1994), 49.

4. Wayne Suttles, ed., *Northwest Coast*, vol. 7, *Handbook of the North American Indians*, ed. William Sturtevant (Washington, D.C.: Smithsonian Institution, 1990), 561–62.

5. Ezra Bowen, ed., *The Indians*, with text by Benjamin Capps, in Old West Series, ed. George Constable (New York: Time-Life Books, 1973), 86.

6. Fleischner, 40; George Daniels, ed., *The Spanish West*, in Old West Series, ed. George Constable (New York: Time-Life Books, 1976), 59.

7. Werner, 23.

8. Robert Bennett, comp., *We'll All Go Home in the Spring: Personal Accounts and Adventures Told by the Pioneers of the West* (Walla Walla, Wash.: Pioneer Press, 1984), 28.

9. Werner, 152.

10. Masterson, 55–56, 53.

11. Ronan, 42–44.

12. Joanna Stratton, *Pioneer Women: Voices from the Kansas Frontier* (New York: Simon and Schuster, 1981), 111–12.

13. Stratton, 114.

14. Stratton, 114–15.

15. *Rutland (Vt.) Herald*, June 18, 1996; Werner, 21.

16. Stratton, 121–23.

17. James Brooks, " 'This Evil Extends Especially to the Feminine Sex': Captivity and Identity in New Mexico, 1700–1846," in Jameson and Armitage, 100, 99.

18. Daniels, *Spanish West*, 136, 181, 186.

19. J. M. Guinn, *Historical and Biographical Record of Los Angeles and Vicinity* (Chicago: Chapman, 1901), 66.

20. Karin Goudy, "Life in a Boom Town—Oatman, Arizona," in J. Michael Canty and Michael Greeley, eds., *History of Mining in Arizona* (Tucson: Mining Club of Southwest Arizona, 1987), 153.

21. Elliott West, "Beyond Baby Doe: Child Rearing on the Mining Frontier," in Susan Armitage and Elizabeth Jameson, eds., *The Women's West* (Norman: University of Oklahoma Press, 1987), 188.

22. Ronan, 41, 55–56.

23. Eleanor Ferris Patten, "Trailing the Iron Horse," a reminiscence in the Patten Family Papers, 1895–96, Montana State University Special Collections, collection 2339,

box 1, file 16, pp. 5 and 6.

24. Patten, 6–7.

25. Patten, 5.

26. Ronald Takaki, *A Different Mirror: A History of Multicultural America* (Boston: Little, Brown, 1993), 185.

27. "Child Labor in California," *Labor Clarion*, April 13, 1906.

28. Dorothy Hoobler and Thomas Hoobler, *The Chinese American Family Album* (New York: Oxford University Press, 1994), 69–70; Elodie Hogan, "Children of the Streets," *Californian Illustrated*, September 1893, 517–26, (quotation, 525–26).

29. Dee Brown, *The American West* (New York: Scribner's, 1994), 169.

30. Katz, 74–75; Phyllis Smith, *The Gallatin Valley: A History* (Helena, Mont.: Falcon Press, 1997), 91.

31. Deal and McDonald, 156–57.

32. Masterson, 54–55.

33. Kaia Lien Cosgriff interview by Donna Gray, January 8, 1987 (transcript privately held).

34. Hampsten, *Settlers' Children*, 45.

35. Elizabeth Hampsten, "The Nehers and the Martins in North Dakota, 1909–1911," in Lillian Schlissel, Byrd Gibbens, and Elizabeth Hampsten, *Far from Home: Families of the Westward Journey* (New York: Schocken Books, 1989), 182, 187, 192.

36. Ray Calkins, comp., *Looking Back from the Hill: Recollections of Butte People* (Butte, Mont.: Butte/Silver Bow Historical Society, 1982), 7–8.

37. Hampsten, *Settlers' Children*, 16.

38. Pearl Anderson Granner, "This I Remember," unpublished manuscript held by Dr. L. Marilyn Stinson of St. Joseph, Minn.

39. Hampsten, *Settlers' Children*, 152.

40. *Bozeman (Mont.) Daily Chronicle*, April 19, 1998.

41. West, "Beyond Baby Doe," 186; Peavy and Smith, *Women in Waiting*, 113, 127.

42. West, "Beyond Baby Doe," 186.

43. *Rutland (Vt.) Herald*, June 18, 1996.

44. Harriet Otto, *For You Know That Wyoming Will Be Your New Home* (Cheyenne: Wyoming State Museum Volunteers, 1990), 5.

45. Masterson, 42; Cosgriff interview.

46. Lois Barton, *Spencer Butte Pioneers: 100 Years on the Sunny Side of the Butte, 1850–1950* (Eugene, Ore.: Spencer Butte Press, 1982), 11.

47. Barton, 70–71.

48. Hampsten, *Settlers' Children*, 70.

49. Hampsten, *Settlers' Children*, 71.

50. Cosgriff interview.

The Family Circle: Frontier Children within the Home

1. The Great Mystery, or Wakantanka, is a Sioux designation. Utley, 7.

2. Stratton, 144; Gloria Miranda, "Hispano-Mexican Childrearing Practices in pre-American Santa Barbara," *Southern California Quarterly* 65 (Winter 1986): 307–20, (quotation, 309).

3. Jay David, ed., *The American Indian: The First Victim* (New York: William Morrow, 1972), 110.

4. Utley, 5; Fleischner, 25.

5. Bowen, 86; Evelyn Toynton, *Growing Up in America, 1830–1860* (Brookfield, Conn.: Millbrook Press, 1995), 35; d'Azevedo, 347; Wayne Dennis, *The Hopi Child* (New York: Arno, 1972), 101.

6. d'Azevedo, 349–50, 347.

7. d'Azevedo, 270, 351–52; *Cycles of Life*, 33–34.

8. Bowen, 86; Fleischner, 28.

9. Bowen, 86.

10. Fleischner, 26; d'Azevedo, 403; Suttles, 277.

11. Lillie Fergus Maury to Pamelia Fergus, January 15, 1877, James Fergus Papers, K. Ross Toole Archives, Mansfield Library, University of Montana, Missoula.

12. Family story shared by audience member with Peavy and Smith, Tillamook, Oregon, September 1994.

13. Hampsten, *Settlers' Children*, 15.

14. Hampsten, *Settlers' Children*, 211, 213.

15. Masterson, 81.

16. Elliott West, "Children of the Plains Frontier," in West and Petrik, 36.

17. Hoobler and Hoobler, *Mexican American Family Album*, 13–14; Ruth Pelz, *Women of the Wild West: Biographies from Many Cultures* (Seattle: Open Hand Publishing, 1995), 9–10; Daniels, *Spanish West*, 136.

18. Brown, *Hispano Folklife*, 116–17.

19. Brown, *Hispano Folklife*, 119.

20. Bennett, 278–79; Masterson, 53.

21. Utley, 13.

22. Leaphart, 90–91.

23. Cosgriff interview.

24. Stratton, 131–32, 183.

25. Stratton, 132.

26. Cosgriff interview.

27. Urma DeLongTaylor interview by Donna Gray, May 9, 1985 (transcript privately held).

28. Barton, 64–65.

29. Barton, 85.

30. Otto, 12.

31. Dean, 41; Masterson, 78.

32. Judy Alter, *Growing Up in the Old West* (New York: Franklin Watts, 1989), 41; Deal and McDonald, 292; Goudy, 155.

33. Stratton, 133–34.

34. Ronan, 72–73.

35. Calkins, 13.

36. John Kent Folmar, ed., *"This State of Wonders": The Letters of an Iowa Frontier Family, 1858–1861* (Iowa City: University of Iowa Press, 1986), 117.

37. Brown, *Hispano Folklife*, 175–76.

38. Brown, *Hispano Folklife*, 176.

39. Mary Goldsmith Prag, "Early Days" (Berkeley, Calif.: Western Jewish History Center, Judah L. Magnes Museum).

40. Hoobler and Hoobler, *Chinese American Family Album*, 116.

41. Hampsten, *Settlers' Children*, 166, 179.

42. Hampsten, *Settlers' Children*, 45.

43. Masterson, 7.

44. Hampsten, "Nehers and Martins," 191–92.

45. Craig Doherty and Katherine Doherty, *The Apaches and Navajos* (New York: Franklin Watts, 1989) 24, 27.

46. Angela Louise Abair, "'A Mustard Seed in Montana: Recollections of the First Indian Mission in Montana,' Ursuline Nuns on the Northern Cheyenne Indian Reservation," ed. by Orlan Svingen, *Montana The Magazine of Western History* 34 (Spring 1984): 16–31 (quotation, 23–24).

47. Hampsten, *Settlers' Children*, 76.

48. Mary Agnes McCann, S.C., *The History of Mother Seton's Daughters, 1809–1923* (Sisters of Charity of Cincinnati, Ohio, 1923), 3, 206.

49. Dean, 42.

50. *Butte Miner*, November 8, 1900, and July 26, 1908. The Paul Clark Home is operated today as the Ronald McDonald Family Place (correspondence from Ellen Crain, Butte–Silver Bow Public Archives, April 27, 1998).

51. Edith Pollock Schumacher interview by Donna Gray, January 24, 1976.

52. Leaphart, 85; West, "Beyond Baby Doe," 187–88.

53. Leaphart, 88.

54. Leaphart, 87.

55. Takaki, 169–70; Daniels, *Spanish West*, 181.

56. Takaki, 169.

57. Hampsten, *Settlers' Children*, 32.

58. *Cycles of Life*, 27.

59. Utley, 5–6, 202, 255, 270, 302.

60. Brown, *Hispano Folklife*, 7–8.

61. Takaki, 247.

62. David Beesley, "From Chinese to Chinese American," *California History*, September 1988: 168–79, 176, 177.

Blurred Boundaries: Frontier Children at Work and Play

1. Hoobler and Hoobler, *Chinese American Family Album*, 12; Brown, *Hispano Folklife*, 126; Elliott West, "Child's Play: Tradition and Adaptation on the Frontier," *Montana The Magazine of Western History* 38 (Winter 1988): 2–15, 9–10.

2. Bowen, 86.

3. d'Azevedo, 273; Granville Stuart, *Pioneering in Montana: The Making of a State, 1864–1887* (Lincoln: University of Nebraska Press, 1977), 52; Suttles, 405.

4. Fleischner, 23, 35–36; d'Azevedo, 311; Bowen, 88.

5. Fleischner, 35–36; Bowen, 87–88; d'Azevedo, 383; Gridley, 54–55.

6. *The Woman's Way* (Alexandria, Va.: Time-Life Books, 1995), 25–26.

7. Bowen, 87–88; *Cycles of Life*, 47.

8. Doherty and Doherty, 36–37.

9. West, "Child's Play," 12.

10. Peavy and Smith, *Women in Waiting*, 231.

11. Hampsten, *Settlers' Children*, 54; Cosgriff interview.

12. Brown, *Hispanic Folklife*, 8–9.

13. Cosgriff interview.

14. Otto, 22.

15. Taylor interview.

16. Hampsten, *Settlers' Children*, 54–55.

17. Folmar, 61–62.

18. Masterson, 6.

19. Taylor interview; Otto, 1.

20. Calkins, 12; Otto, 19.

21. Peavy and Smith, *Pioneer Women*, 86.

22. Reichman Family Papers, 1902–1944, collection 893, Merrill G. Burlingame Special Collections, Montana State University Libraries, Bozeman.

23. Leaphart, 87; West, "Beyond Baby Doe," 188.

24. Otto, 13.

25. Calkins, 17 ff.

26. Calkins, 20; Leaphart, 87.

27. Hampsten, *Settlers' Children*, 20; West, "Child's Play," 6.

28. Alter, 21; Glenda Riley, *Frontierswomen: The Iowa Experience* (Ames: Iowa State University Press, 1982), 84.

29. Alter, 24, 27–28.

30. Hampsten, *Settlers' Children*, 55; Stratton, 145–46.

31. Hampsten, *Settlers' Children*, 55; Folmar, xxvi.

32. Hampsten, *Settlers' Children*, 14.

33. Hampsten, *Settlers' Children*, 14, 18–19.

34. Stratton, 146; Dean, 38.

35. West, "Children on the Plains Frontier," 31; Hampsten, *Settlers' Children*, 55.

36. Stratton, 145.

37. West, "Children on the Plains Frontier," 38; Dean, 38.

38. West, "Children on the Plains Frontier," 28; Stratton, 145.

39. Toynton, 30; Riley, 84.

40. Liahna Babener, "Recollections of Childhood on the Midwestern Frontier," in West and Petrik, eds. (quotations, 308, 310); West, "Children on the Plains Frontier," 35.

41. West, "Children on the Plains Frontier," 30.

42. West, *Growing Up with the Country*, xi.

43. West, "Child's Play," 7; West, "Children on the Plains Frontier," 26.

44. Deal and McDonald, 54.

45. Otto, 28.

46. West, "Children on the Plains Frontier," 37, 31.

47. Brown, *Hispano Folklife*, 9.

48. Hampsten, "Nehers and Martins," 221–23.

49. Barton, 80–81.

50. Otto, 23.

51. Richard White, *"It's Your Misfortune and None of My Own": A New History of the American West* (Norman: University of Oklahoma Press, 1991), 278.

52. Calkins, 21, 12.

53. Hogan, 518.

54. Hogan, 521.

55. *Labor Clarion*, April 13, 1906.

56. *Labor Clarion*, April 13, 1906.

57. Ronan, 48–50.

58. Ronan, 62.

All the World's a School:
The Education of Frontier Children

1. Hampsten, *Settlers' Children*, 6–7, 36.

2. *Cycles of Life*, 42; Stuart, 53.

3. *Woman's Way*, 266; Fleischner, 28; Utley, 11.

4. Suttles, 405; *Woman's Way*, 24–25.

5. Doherty and Doherty, 55; Gridley, 47–48; Fleischner, 31.

6. Fleischner, 31.

7. David, 72–73.

8. Peter Nabokov, *Indian Running* (Santa Barbara, Calif.: Capra Press, 1981), 136–37.

9. *Cycles of Life*, 43–45; Nabokov, 137.

10. *Woman's Way*, 26.

11. Ramona Ford, "Native American Women: Changing Statuses, Changing Interpretations," in Jameson and Armitage, 58; Hiner and Hawes, 170.

12. Michael Coleman, "Motivations of Indian Children at Missionary and U.S. Government Schools, 1860–1918: A Study through Published Reminiscences," *Montana The*

Magazine of Western History 40 (Winter 1990): 30–45, 32; *From Trout Creek to Gravy High: The Boarding School Experience at Wind River*, exhibit catalog, Warm Valley (Wyo.) Historical Project, 1992, unpaged, with an introductory essay by Peter Iverson.

13. *From Trout Creek*; Coleman, 32.

14. Coleman, 35; *From Trout Creek*.

15. *From Trout Creek*, Iverson essay.

16. Coleman, 35.

17. *From Trout Creek*, Iverson essay.

18. Gridley, 81.

19. Dean, 40.

20. *From Trout Creek*, Iverson essay.

21. *From Trout Creek*, Iverson essay.

22. *From Trout Creek*; Coleman, 30; Dean, 40.

23. Gridley, 81–82; David, 53–54.

24. David, 146; Coleman, 43.

25. Alter, 43–44.

26. Hampsten, *Settlers' Children*, 40; Riley, 137–38.

27. Riley, 137.

28. Peavy and Smith, *Women in Waiting*, 356.

29. Dean, 38; Masterson, 67.

30. Masterson, 67.

31. Deal and McDonald, 54.

32. Deal and McDonald, 54; Riley, 137, 138.

33. Hampsten, *Settlers' Children*, 55–56.

34. Polly Welts Kaufman, *Women Teachers on the Frontier* (New Haven: Yale University Press, 1984), 215–24.

35. White, 313; Hampsten, *Settlers' Children*, 35.

36. Calkins, 12.

37. Ronan, 52–53.

38. Masterson, 5–6.

39. Calkins, 13.

40. Riley, 137; Hampsten, *Settlers' Children*, 40.

41. Riley, 138.

42. Otto, 25.

43. Folmar, 62.

44. Riley, 138; Otto, 25.

45. Ronan, 54.

46. Riley, 137.

47. Linda Peavy and Sally Babcock, eds. *Canyon Cookery* (Bozeman, Mont.: Bridger Canyon Women's Club, 1978), 96–97; Masterson, 69.

48. Bennett, 319–20.

49. Miranda, 315, 316.

50. Riley, 92; Meltzer, 107; Hoobler and Hoobler, *Chinese American Family Album*, 70.

51. Katz, 137.

52. James, 624; Pelz, 45–46; Gae Whitney Canfield, *Sarah*

Winnemucca of the Northern Paiutes (Norman: University of Oklahoma Press, 1983), 30–31.

53. Daniels, *Spanish West*, 131; McCann, 3, 131; Ruth Barnes Moynihan, Cynthia Russett, and Laurie Crumpacker, eds., *Second to None: A Documentary History of American Women*, vol. 1, *From the Sixteenth Century to 1865* (Lincoln: University of Nebraska Press, 1993), 363.

54. White, 313.

55. White, 313; Barton, 87.

Passages:
Coming of Age on the Frontier

1. *Cycles of Life*, 51; Suttles, 405, 277.

2. Bowen, 88.

3. *Cycles of Life*, 70–71.

4. Toynton, 38; *Woman's Way*, 26, 29.

5. *Woman's Way*, 29; d'Azevedo, 380, 311–12.

6. Bowen, 88; Stuart, 52–53.

7. Nabokov, 139.

8. Toynton, 38.

9. *Indians of the Plains*, 48; Bowen, 87.

10. Utley, 5–17.

11. *Indians of the Plains*, 48.

12. Olive Martin interview by Linda Peavy, June 4, 1986.

13. Carol Fairbanks, "Lives of Girls and Women on the Canadian and American Prairie," *International Journal of Women's Studies* 2: 452–72 (quotation, 456); Hampsten, "Nehers and Martins," 192.

14. Ronan, 70–71.

15. Stefoff, 71; Masterson, 60–62.

16. Miranda, 313; Genaro Padilla, "'Yo Sola Aprendi': Mexican Women's Personal Narratives from Nineteenth Century California," in Jameson and Armitage, 194–95.

17. Calkins, 17.

18. Peavy and Smith, *Pioneer Women*, 102.

19. Hampsten, *Settlers' Children*, 44–46.

20. Peavy and Smith, *Pioneer Women*, 101.

21. Peavy and Smith, *Women in Waiting*, 120, 121, 112–13, 106, 123.

22. Peavy and Smith, *Women in Waiting*, 261, 232.

23. Bennett, 147–50.

Below: *The Sweet Pea Festival, held in Bozeman, Montana, every August to celebrate the region's commercial success at pea growing, included activities for children as well as adults. The winner of the 1913 doll buggy competition was Doris Thompson, second child from the right.*

Acknowledgments

American Heritage Center, University of Wyoming: **142** (Knight Collection, B-31,570, neg. 28127).

Arizona Historical Society, Tucson: **66** (AHS #2138).

Bancroft Library, University of California, Berkeley: **72**

Brigham Young University, Provo, Utah, Harold B. Lee Library, Photographic Archives: **14** (G. E. Anderson #30695).

California Historical Society, San Francisco: **ii, 49 (bottom)** (detail from FN-10744), **99** (FN-26284).

California School for the Deaf Historical Museum, Fremont, California: **134 (bottom)**.

California State Library, Sacramento, California History Room: **48 (bottom)** (#25,215), **111** coal picker (#25,216) and wood gatherer (#25,218).

California State Parks: **37** (DPR #090-840 [311-83]), **75 bottom)** (DPR #311-17).

Canadian Museum of Civilization, Hull, Quebec: **138** (MCC/CMC #27097).

Carnegie Branch Library for Local History, Boulder (Colorado) Historical Society Collection: **88** (#141-5-12), **103 (top)** (#141-7-32).

Church of Jesus Christ of Latter-day Saints, Historical Department, Salt Lake City: **30–31** (#P1300/188).

Daughters of the Republic of Texas Library at the Alamo: **46 (bottom)** (detail from #CN96.285).

Denver Public Library, Western History Collection: **viii** (#F32936), **17** (#X-11000121), **20, 21** (#X-11000223), **38** (X-11682), **46 (top)** (#MCC-485), **48 (top)** (#14510), **71 (bottom)** (#NS-758), **126** (X-13959), **134 (top)** (X-2825).

Douglas County (Oregon) Museum: **148** (#N16275), **60** (detail from GP5/7.346), **106 (bottom)** (#GP4/5.39), **104 (bottom)** (#N4158).

Janice Romney Dunbar: **64, 68 (top)**.

Gallatin County (Montana) Historical Society: **73 (bottom)** (#P553N).

Greybull (Wyoming) Museum: **113 (top)**.

Iris Hancock: **ii, 76**.

Homesteader Museum, Powell, Wyoming: **75 (top), 128 (bottom)**.

Huntington Library, San Marino, California: **47 (top)**.

Idaho State Historical Society, Boise: **85** (#65-128.38), **135** (#79-95.30).

Kansas State Historical Society, Topeka: **iii, 32** (#He.56), **78 (top)** (#ATSF 5/21.148), **124 (top)** (#FK2.T1.76).

Lane County Historical Museum, Eugene, Oregon: **70** (#L74-754), **100 (bottom)** (#L72-226c), **104 (bottom)** (#L78-1021A), **92 (right)** (#L83-39F), **98** (#L79-1100).

Library of Congress, Washington, D.C.: **23** (#USZ62-26365).

Minnesota Historical Society, St. Paul: **44 (right)** (photo by Whitney), **91** (photo by Edwin R. Baker; #GV1.1/p87), **94 (top)** (photo by Harriet Friedmann Schmidt Schroeck; #GV8.2/p46), **144** (photo by Ross Daniels; #GT1.7/r4).

Missouri Historical Society, St. Louis: **140** (Wo Haw 41, Art Acc. 1882.18.41).

Montana Historical Society, Helena: **xii–1** (Haynes Foundation Collection, #H-1825, **18 (bottom)** (PAc 76-41), **iv, 10 (bottom)** (#941-871), **10 (top), 7** (#943-788), **15** (#981-030), **39** (#981-037), **43 (bottom)** (Haynes Foundation Collection, #H-1699), **50** (PAc 90-87), **56** (lot 8, box 1/4.08), **59 (top)** (Haynes Foundation Collection, #H-4758), **53 (top)** (PAc 75-51.2), **64 (top)** (Deem Collection, #40), **73 (top)** (#949-941), **74 (top)** (#PAc 83-78), **80** (#953-389), **81** (#M900-253), **82 (bottom)** (#944-430), **82 (top)** (#981-245), **90 (top left)** (#981-160), **94 (bottom)** (PAc 90-87, 61-8), **96 (top)** (PAc 90-87, 3-18), **97** (PAc 75-51.7), **101 (bottom)** (Haynes Foundation Collection, #H-3285), **102 (top)** (PAc 82-3), **113 (bottom)** (PAc 87-13), **92 (bottom)** (#942-543), **iii, 92 (top left)** (#981-135), **119** (#947-400), **120** (#947-409), **127 (bottom)** (Haynes Foundation Collection, #H-602), **130** (#950-880), **132 (top)** (Haynes Foundation Collection, #H-4399), **131** (#957-628), **139 (top)** (#981-124), **141** (PAc 90-87, 57-c), **146 (top)** (PAc 82-62.1295), **146 (bottom)** (#953-060), **104 (top)** PAc 95-46.8).

Montana State University, Bozeman, Merrill G. Burlingame Special Collections: **4 (bottom)** (Picture Collection, #197), **24** (Picture Collection, #50), **57 (bottom)** (#F739.B8.B89), **53 (bottom)** (#199), **77** (Merrill G. Burlingame Papers, collection 2245, #162), **115** (E99.C92I52 1895z), **128 (top)** (Edna Tracy White Papers, 1869-1908, #1332), **143 (top)** (Picture Collection, #225).

Museum of New Mexico, Santa Fe: **117 (bottom)** (photo by H. F. Robinson; #4791), **143 (bottom)** (photo by Jesse L. Nusbaum; #61817).

Museum of the Rockies, Bozeman, Montana: **33, 154** (83.103.02).

National Frontier Trails Center, Independence, Missouri: **36, 55 (bottom)**.

National Park Service, Yellowstone National Park: **40 (bottom)** (#YELL 37742).

Nebraska State Historical Society, Lincoln: **57 (top)** (#C689-45), **69** (RG2035-137), **102 (bottom)** (#C521:10-72), **iii, 103 (bottom)** (RG2301-2c); from the Solomon D. Butcher Collection, **5** (RG2608-3535), **43** (RG2608-3359), **51** (RG2608-1345), **107** (RG2906-1947).

Newberry Library, Chicago, Edward E. Ayer Collection: **90 (bottom)**.

New York Public Library: **40 (top)** (Branch Libraries, Picture Collection), **137** (reproduced from George Catlin, *Souvenir of the North American Indians* [London, 1850], pl. 124, in Rare Books Division, Astor, Lenox, and Tilden Foundations).

North Dakota Institute for Regional Studies, NDSU, Fargo, Fred Hulstrand History in Pictures Collection: **54 (bottom), 59 (bottom)**.

Northwest College, Powell, Wyoming: **105 (top)**.

North Wind Picture Archives: **35, 118 (top), 118 (bottom)**.

Oregon Historical Society, Portland: **55 (top)** (#OrHi 36118), **63 (left)** (#OrHi 35788), **61** (#CN8785), **93 (top)** (#016375), **109 (top)** (OrHi 6546, #869).

Peter E. Palmquist Collection: **6 (top)** (photo by A. W. Ericson).

Kirk Pearce Collection, Lebanon, Missouri: **78 (bottom)**.

San Diego Historical Society: **124 (bottom)** (Ticor Collection, #2875).

Santa Maria Valley (California) Historical Society: **9, 65** (#90-P-97), **71 (top)** (#93-Re-11).

Seaver Center for Western History Research, Los Angeles County Museum of Natural History: **83, 110** (Coll. 4170).

Smithsonian Institution: **89** (#75-11740), **117 (top left)** (#NAA 76-13355), **121** (#3421-B-65).

South Dakota State Historical Society—State Archives: **114**.

Stanford University Libraries, Department of Special Collections: **49 (top)**.

State Historical Society of North Dakota, Bismark: **84 (left, right)**, photos by David H. Barry of Standing Holy (#A-1679) and Crow Foot (#22-h-157).

Dr. L. Marilyn Stinson: **67, 129**.

Sutter's Fort, California Department of Parks and Recreation: **27** (photo by Nikki Pahl).

University of Kansas Libraries, Kansas Collection: **11 (left)** (Pennell Collection #312).

University of Montana—Missoula, K. Ross Toole Archives: **2** (#778-111), **ii, 13** (#86-0168), **54 (top)** (#84-3), **58** (#94-3433), **52 (bottom)** (#72-840), **63 (right)** (#92-295), **74 (bottom)** (#82-296), **86 (top)** (#94-3454), **86 (bottom)** (94-3535), **90 (top right)** (#78-112), **95** (#92-134), **100 (top)** (#75-252), **104 (middle)** (#75-218), **122** (#72-833).

University of Oklahoma Libraries, Norman, Western History Collections: **68 (bottom)** (DDS #548).

University of Oregon Library System, Eugene, Division of Special Collections and University Archives, Stearns and Chenoweth Collection: **4 (top), 116** (photo by Roy Andrews).

University of Southern California Library, Los Angeles, Department of Special Collections, Title Insurance and Trust Photograph Collection, California Historical Society Collection: **12** (# 2138), **52 (top)** (#4632), **127 (top)** (#6508), **133** (#2025), **139 (bottom)** (#4621).

Utah State Historical Society, Salt Lake City: **19** (#10106).

Washington State Historical Society, Tacoma: **42** (#1.01,001).

West Point Museum Collections, United States Military Academy: **3**.

Woolaroc Museum, Bartlesville, Oklahoma: **16**.

World Museum of Mining, Butte, Montana: **47 (bottom)** (book 51, #1283), **101 (top)** (book 20, #306), **147** (book 19, #1588).

Wyoming Division of Cultural Resources, Wyoming State Archives, Cheyenne: **6 (bottom, 25** (#25384), **8 (top)** (#415), **vi, 62** (#359), **93 (bottom)** (Kennedy Collection, #20), **96 (bottom)** (#19044), **105 (bottom)** (#14521), **106 (top)** (#5239), **108** (#13763), **117 (top right)** (#395), **132 (right)** (#19501), **136** (#49).

Index

Boldfaced page numbers refer to photos and/or captions.

INDEX